LETTERS
TO MALCOLM:
CHIEFLY
ON
PRAYER

BY C. S. LEWIS

LETTERS
TO MALCOLM:
CHIEFLY
ON
PRAYER

C. S. LEWIS

A Harvest Book
Harcourt Brace & Company
San Diego   New York   London

Library of Congress Catalog Card Number: 64-11536

ISBN 0-15-650880-X (pbk.)

Printed in the United States of America
R T U S

LETTERS
TO MALCOLM:
CHIEFLY
ON
PRAYER

I AM all in favour of your idea that we should go back to our old plan of having a more or less set subject—an *agendum*—for our letters. When we were last separated the correspondence languished for lack of it. How much better we did in our undergraduate days with our interminable letters on the *Republic,* and classical metres, and what was then the "new" psychology! Nothing makes an absent friend so present as a disagreement.

Prayer, which you suggest, is a subject that is a good deal in my mind. I mean, private prayer. If you were thinking of corporate prayer, I won't play. There is no subject in the world (always excepting sport) on which I have less to say than liturgiology. And the almost nothing which I have to say may as well be disposed of in this letter.

I think our business as laymen is to take what we are given and make the best of it. And I think we should find this a great deal easier if what we were given was always and everywhere the same.

To judge from their practice, very few Anglican clergymen take this view. It looks as if they believed people can be lured to go to church by incessant brightenings, lightenings, lengthenings, abridgements, simplifications, and complications of the service. And it is probably true that a new, keen vicar will usually be able to form within his parish a minority who are in favour of his innovations. The majority, I believe, never are. Those who remain—many give up churchgoing altogether—merely endure.

Is this simply because the majority are hide-bound? I think not. They have a good reason for their conservatism. Novelty, simply as such, can have only an entertainment value. And they don't go to church to be entertained. They go to *use* the service, or, if you prefer, to *enact* it. Every service is a structure of acts and words through which we receive a sacrament, or repent, or supplicate, or adore. And it enables us to do these things best—if you like, it "works" best—when, through long familiarity, we don't have to think about it. As long as you notice, and have to count, the steps, you are not yet dancing but only learning to dance. A good shoe is a shoe you don't notice. Good reading becomes possible when you need not consciously think about eyes, or light, or print, or spelling. The perfect church service would be one we were almost unaware of; our attention would have been on God.

But every novelty prevents this. It fixes our attention on the service itself; and thinking about worship is a different

4

thing from worshipping. The important question about the Grail was "for what does it serve?" " 'Tis mad idolatry that makes the service greater than the god."

A still worse thing may happen. Novelty may fix our attention not even on the service but on the celebrant. You know what I mean. Try as one may to exclude it, the question "What on earth is he up to now?" will intrude. It lays one's devotion waste. There is really some excuse for the man who said, "I wish they'd remember that the charge to Peter was Feed my sheep; not Try experiments on my rats, or even, Teach my performing dogs new tricks."

Thus my whole liturgiological position really boils down to an entreaty for permanence and uniformity. I can make do with almost any kind of service whatever, if only it will stay put. But if each form is snatched away just when I am beginning to feel at home in it, then I can never make any progress in the art of worship. You give me no chance to acquire the trained habit—*habito dell'arte.*

It may well be that some variations which seem to me merely matters of taste really involve grave doctrinal differences. But surely not all? For if grave doctrinal differences are really as numerous as variations in practice, then we shall have to conclude that no such thing as the Church of England exists. And anyway, the Liturgical Fidget is not a purely Anglican phenomenon; I have heard Roman Catholics complain of it too.

And that brings me back to my starting point. The business of us laymen is simply to endure and make the best of it. Any tendency to a passionate preference for one type of service must be regarded simply as a temptation. Partisan "Churchmanships" are my *bête noire.* And if we avoid them, may we not possibly perform a very useful function? The shepherds go off, "everyone to his own way," and vanish over diverse points of the horizon. If the sheep huddle patiently together and go on bleating, might they finally recall the shepherds? (Haven't English victories sometimes been won by the rank and file in spite of the generals?)

As to the words of the service—liturgy in the narrower sense—the question is rather different. If you have a vernacular liturgy you must have a changing liturgy: otherwise it will finally be vernacular only in name. The ideal of "timeless English" is sheer nonsense. No living language can be timeless. You might as well ask for a motionless river.

I think it would have been best, if it were possible, that necessary change should have occurred gradually and (to most people) imperceptibly; here a little and there a little; one obsolete word replaced in a century—like the gradual change of spelling in successive editions of Shakespeare. As things are, we must reconcile ourselves, if we can also reconcile government, to a new Book.

If we were—I thank my stars I'm not—in a position to give its authors advice, would you have any advice to give them? Mine could hardly go beyond unhelpful cautions: "Take care. It is so easy to break eggs without making omelettes."

Already our liturgy is one of the very few remaining elements of unity in our hideously divided Church. The good to be done by revision needs to be very great and very certain before we throw that away. Can you imagine any new Book which will not be a source of new schism?

Most of those who press for revision seem to wish that it should serve two purposes: that of modernising the language in the interests of intelligibility, and that of doctrinal improvement. Ought the two operations—each painful and each dangerous—to be carried out at the same time? Will the patient survive?

What are the agreed doctrines which are to be embodied in the new Book and how long will agreement on them continue? I ask with trepidation because I read a man the other day who seemed to wish that everything in the old book which was inconsistent with orthodox Freudianism should be deleted.

For whom are we to cater in revising the language? A country parson I know asked his sexton what he understood by *indifferently* in the phrase "truly and indifferently administer justice." The man replied, "It means making no difference between one chap and another." "And what would it mean if it said *impartially?*" asked the parson. "Don't know. Never heard of it," said the sexton. Here, you see, we have a change intended to make things easier. But it does so neither for the educated, who understand *indifferently* already, nor for the wholly uneducated, who don't understand *impartially*. It helps only some middle area of the congregation which may not even be a majority. Let us hope the revisers will prepare for their work by a prolonged empirical study of popular speech as it actually is, not as we (*a priori*) assume it to be. How many scholars know (what I discovered by accident) that when uneducated people say *impersonal* they sometimes mean *incorporeal?*

What of expressions which are archaic but not unintelligible? ("Be ye lift up.") I find that people re-act to archaism most diversely. It antagonises some; makes what is said unreal. To others, not necessarily more learned, it is highly numinous and a real aid to devotion. We can't please both.

I know there must be change. But is this the right moment? Two signs of the right moment occur to me. One would be a unity among us which enabled the Church—not some momentarily triumphant party—to speak through the new work with a united voice. The other would be the manifest presence, somewhere in the Church, of the specifically literary talent needed for composing a good prayer. Prose needs to be not only very good but very good in a very special way, if it is to stand up to reiterated reading aloud. Cranmer may have his defects as a theologian; as a stylist, he can play all the moderns, and many of his predecessors, off the field. I don't see either sign at the moment.

Yet we all want to be tinkering. Even I would gladly see "Let your light so shine before men" removed from the offertory. It sounds, in that context, so like an exhortation to do our alms that they may be seen by men.

I'd meant to follow up what you say about Rose Macaulay's letters, but that must wait till next week.

II

I CAN'T understand why you say that my view of church services is "man-centred" and too concerned with "mere edification." How does this follow from anything I said? Actually my ideas about the sacrament would probably be called "magical" by a good many modern theologians. Surely, the more fully one believes that a strictly supernatural event takes place, the less one can attach any great importance to the dress, gestures, and position of the priest? I agree with you that he is there not only to edify the people but to glorify God. But how can a man glorify God by placing obstacles in the way of the people? Especially if the slightest element of "clerical one-upmanship"—I owe the phrase to a cleric—underlies some of his eccentricities? How right is that passage in the *Imitation* where the celebrant is told, "Consult not your own devotion but the edification of your flock." I've forgotten how the Latin runs.

Now about the Rose Macaulay *Letters*. Like you, I was staggered by this continual search for more and more prayers. If she were merely collecting them as *objets d'art* I could understand it; she was a born collector. But I get the impression that she collected them in order to use them; that her whole prayer-life depended on what we may call "ready-made" prayers—prayers written by other people.

But though, like you, staggered, I was not, like you, repelled. One reason is that I had—and you hadn't—the luck to meet her. Make no mistake. She was the right sort; one of the most fully civilised people I ever knew. The other reason, as I have so often told you, is that you are a bigot. Broaden your mind, Malcolm, broaden your mind! It takes all sorts to make a world; or a church. This may be even truer of a church. If grace perfects nature it must expand all our natures into the full richness of the diversity which God intended when He made them, and Heaven will display far more variety than Hell. "One fold" doesn't mean "one pool." Cultivated roses and daffodils are no more alike than wild roses and daffodils. What pleased me most about a Greek Orthodox mass I once attended was that there seemed to be no prescribed behaviour for the congregation. Some stood, some knelt, some sat, some walked; one crawled about the floor like a caterpillar. And the beauty of it was that nobody took the slightest notice of what anyone else was doing. I wish we Anglicans would follow their example. One meets people who are perturbed because someone in the next pew does, or does not, cross himself. They oughtn't even to have seen, let alone censured. "Who art thou that judgest Another's servant?"

I don't doubt, then, that Rose Macaulay's method was the

right one for her. It wouldn't be for me, any more than for you.

All the same, I am not quite such a purist in this matter as I used to be. For many years after my conversion I never used any ready-made forms except the Lord's Prayer. In fact I tried to pray without words at all—not to verbalise the mental acts. Even in praying for others I believe I tended to avoid their names and substituted mental images of them. I still think the prayer without words is the best—if one can really achieve it. But I now see that in trying to make it my daily bread I was counting on a greater mental and spiritual strength than I really have. To pray successfully without words one needs to be "at the top of one's form." Otherwise the mental acts become merely imaginative or emotional acts—and a fabricated emotion is a miserable affair. When the golden moments come, when God enables one really to pray without words, who but a fool would reject the gift? But He does not give it—anyway not to me—day in, day out. My mistake was what Pascal, if I remember rightly, calls "Error of Stoicism": thinking we can do always what we can do sometimes.

And this, you see, makes the choice between ready-made prayers and one's own words rather less important for me than it apparently is for you. For me words are in any case secondary. They are only an anchor. Or, shall I say, they are the movements of a conductor's baton: not the music. They serve to canalise the worship or penitence or petition which might without them—such are our minds—spread into wide and shallow puddles. It does not matter very much who first put them together. If they are our own words they will soon, by unavoidable repetition, harden into a formula. If they are someone else's, we shall continually pour into them our own meaning.

At present—for one's practice changes and, I think, ought to change—I find it best to make "my own words" the staple but introduce a modicum of the ready-made.

Writing to you, I need not stress the importance of the home-made staple. As Solomon said at the dedication of the temple, each man who prays knows "the plague of his own heart." Also, the comforts of his own heart. No other creature is identical with me; no other situation identical with mine. Indeed, I myself and my situation are in continual change. A ready-made form can't serve for my intercourse with God any more than it could serve for my intercourse with you.

This is obvious. Perhaps I shan't find it so easy to persuade you that the ready-made modicum has also its use: for me, I mean—I'm not suggesting rules for anyone else in the whole world.

First, it keeps me in touch with "sound doctrine." Left to oneself, one could easily slide away from "the faith once given" into a phantom called "my religion."

Secondly, it reminds me "what things I ought to ask" (perhaps especially when I am praying for other people). The crisis of the present moment, like the nearest telegraph-post, will always loom largest. Isn't there a danger that our great, permanent, objective necessities—often more important—may get crowded out? By the way, that's another thing to be avoided in a revised Prayer Book. "Contemporary problems" may claim an undue share. And the more "up to date" the book is, the sooner it will be dated.

Finally, they provide an element of the ceremonial. On your view, that is just what we don't want. On mine, it is part of what we want. I see what you mean when you say that using ready-made prayers would be like "making love to your own wife out of Petrarch or Donne." (Incidentally

might you not *quote* them—to such a literary wife as Betty?)
The parallel won't do.

I fully agree that the relationship between God and a man
is more private and intimate than any possible relation between two fellow creatures. Yes, but at the same time there
is, in another way, a greater distance between the partici-
pants. We are approaching—well I won't say "the Wholly
Other," for I suspect that is meaningless, but the Unimaginably and Insupportably Other. We ought to be—sometimes
I hope one is—simultaneously aware of closest proximity
and infinite distance. You make things far too snug and con-
fiding. Your erotic analogy needs to be supplemented by "I
fell at His feet as one dead."

I think the "low" church *milieu* that I grew up in did tend to
be too cosily at ease in Sion. My grandfather, I'm told, used
to say that he "looked forward to having some very interest-
ing conversations with St. Paul when he got to heaven." Two
clerical gentlemen talking at ease in a club! It never seemed
to cross his mind that an encounter with St. Paul might be
rather an overwhelming experience even for an Evangelical
clergyman of good family. But when Dante saw the great
apostles in heaven they affected him like *mountains*. There's
lots to be said against devotions to saints; but at least they
keep on reminding us that we are very small people compared with them. How much smaller before their Master?

A few formal, ready-made, prayers serve me as a corrective of—well, let's call it "cheek." They keep one side of
the paradox alive. Of course it is only one side. It would be
better not to be reverent at all than to have a reverence
which denied the proximity.

III

O<small>H</small> for mercy's sake. Not you too! Why, just because I raised an objection to your parallel between prayer and a man making love to his own wife, must you trot out all the old rigmarole about the "holiness" of sex and start lecturing me as if I were a Manichaean? I know that in most circles nowadays one need only mention sex to set everyone in the room emitting this gas. But, I did hope, not you. Didn't I make it plain that I objected to your image solely on the ground of its nonchalance, or presumption?

I'm not saying anything against (or for) "sex." Sex in itself cannot be moral or immoral any more than gravitation or nutrition. The sexual behaviour of human beings can. And like their economic, or political, or agricultural, or parental, or filial behaviour, it is sometimes good and sometimes bad. And the sexual act, when lawful—which means chiefly when consistent with good faith and charity—can, like all other merely natural acts ("whether we eat or drink etc.," as the apostle says), be done to the glory of God, and will then be holy. And like other natural acts it is sometimes so done, and sometimes not. This may be what the poor Bishop of Woolwich was trying to say. Anyway, what more is there to be said? And can we now get this red herring out of the way? I'd be glad if we could; for the moderns have achieved the feat, which I should have thought impossible, of making the whole subject a bore. Poor Aphrodite! they have sand-papered most of the Homeric laughter off her face.

Apparently I have been myself guilty of introducing another red herring by mentioning devotions to saints. I didn't in the least want to go off into a discussion on that subject. There is clearly a theological defence for it; if you can ask for the prayers of the living, why should you not ask for the prayers of the dead? There is clearly also a great danger. In some popular practice we see it leading off into an infinitely silly picture of Heaven as an earthly court where applicants will be wise to pull the right wires, discover the best "channels," and attach themselves to the most influential pressure groups. But I have nothing to do with all this. I am not thinking of adopting the practice myself; and who am I to judge the practices of others? I only hope there'll be no scheme for canonisations in the Church of England. Can you imagine a better hot-bed for yet more divisions between us?

The consoling thing is that while Christendom is divided about the rationality, and even the lawfulness, of praying *to* the saints, we are all agreed about praying *with* them. "With angels and archangels and all the company of heaven." Will you believe it? It is only quite recently I made that quotation a part of my private prayers—I festoon it round "hallowed be Thy name." This, by the way, illustrates what I was saying last week about the uses of ready-made forms. They remind one. And I have found this quotation a great enrichment. One always accepted this *with* theoretically. But it is quite different when one brings it into consciousness at an appropriate moment and wills the association of one's own little twitter with the voice of the great saints and (we hope) of our own dear dead. They may drown some of its uglier qualities and set off any tiny value it has.

You may say that the distinction between the communion of the saints as I find it in that act and full-fledged prayer to saints is not, after all, very great. All the better if so. I sometimes have a bright dream of re-union engulfing us unawares, like a great wave from behind our backs, perhaps at the very moment when our official representatives are still pronouncing it impossible. Discussions usually separate us; actions sometimes unite us.

When I spoke of prayer without words I don't think I meant anything so exalted as what mystics call the "prayer of silence." And when I spoke of being "at the top of one's form" I didn't mean it purely in a spiritual sense. The condition of the body comes in; for I suppose a man may be in a state of grace and yet very sleepy.

And, talking of sleepiness, I entirely agree with you that no one in his senses, if he has any power of ordering his own day, would reserve his chief prayers for bed-time—obviously the worst possible hour for any action which needs concentration. The trouble is that thousands of unfortunate people can hardly find any other. Even for us, who are the lucky ones, it is not always easy. My own plan, when hard pressed, is to seize any time, and place, however unsuitable, in preference to the last waking moment. On a day of travelling—with, perhaps, some ghastly meeting at the end of it—I'd rather pray sitting in a crowded train than put it off till midnight when one reaches a hotel bedroom with aching head and dry throat and one's mind partly in a stupor and partly in a whirl. On other, and slightly less crowded, days a bench in a park, or a back street where one can pace up and down, will do.

A man to whom I was explaining this said, "But why don't you turn into a church?" Partly because, for nine months of the year, it will be freezingly cold, but also because I have had bad luck with churches. No sooner do I enter one and compose my mind than one or other of two things happens. Either someone starts practising the organ. Or else, with resolute tread, there appears from nowhere a pious woman in elastic side-boots, carrying mop, bucket, and dust-pan, and begins beating hassocks and rolling up carpets and doing things to flower vases. Of course (blessings on her) "work is prayer," and her enacted *oratio* is probably worth ten times my spoken one. But it doesn't help mine to become worth more.

When one prays in strange places and at strange times one can't kneel, to be sure. I won't say this doesn't matter. The body ought to pray as well as the soul. Body and soul are both the better for it. Bless the body. Mine has led me into many scrapes, but I've led it into far more. If the imagination were obedient, the appetites would give us very little trouble. And from how much it has saved me! And but for our body one whole realm of God's glory—all that we receive through the senses—would go unpraised. For the beasts can't appreciate it and the angels are, I suppose, pure intelligences. They *understand* colours and tastes better than our greatest scientists; but have they retinas or palates?

I fancy the "beauties of nature" are a secret God has shared with us alone. That may be one of the reasons why we were made—and why the resurrection of the body is an important doctrine.

But I'm being led into a digression; perhaps because I am still smarting under the charge of being a Manichee! The relevant point is that kneeling does matter, but other things matter even more. A concentrated mind and a sitting body make for better prayer than a kneeling body and a mind half asleep. Sometimes these are the only alternatives. (Since the osteoporosis I can hardly kneel at all in most places, myself.)

A clergyman once said to me that a railway compartment, if one has it to oneself, is an extremely good place to pray in "because there is just the right amount of distraction." When I asked him to explain, he said that perfect silence and solitude left one more open to the distractions which come from within, and that a moderate amount of external distraction was easier to cope with. I don't find this so myself, but I can imagine it.

The Jones boy's name is Cyril—though why you find it so important to pray for people by their Christian names I can't imagine. I always assume God knows their surnames as well. I am afraid many people appear in my prayers only as "that old man at Crewe" or "the waitress" or even "that man." One may have lost, or may never have known, their names and yet remember how badly they need to be prayed for.

No letter next week. I shall be in the thick of exams.

IV

O F the two difficulties you mention I think that only one is often a practical problem for believers. The other is in my experience usually raised by people who are attacking Christianity.

The ideal opening for their attacks—if they know the Bible—is the phrase in Philippians about "making your requests known to God." I mean, the words *making known* bring out most clearly the apparent absurdity with which they charge us. We say that we believe God to be omniscient; yet a great deal of prayer seems to consist of giving Him information. And indeed we have been reminded by Our Lord too not to pray as if we forgot the omniscience—"for your heavenly Father knows you need all these things."

This is final against one very silly sort of prayer. I have heard a man offer a prayer for a sick person which really amounted to a diagnosis followed by advice as to how God should treat the patient. And I have heard prayers nominally for peace, but really so concerned for various devices which the petitioner believed to be means to peace, that they were open to the same criticism.

But even when that kind of thing is ruled out, the unbeliever's objection remains. To confess our sins before God is certainly to tell Him what He knows much better than we. And also, any petition is a kind of telling. If it does not strictly exclude the belief that God knows our need, it at least seems to solicit His attention. Some traditional formulae make that implication very clear: "*Hear* us, good Lord"—"O let thine ears consider well the voice of my complaint." As if, though God does not need to be informed, He does need, and even rather frequently, to be reminded. But we cannot really believe that degrees of attention, and therefore of inattention, and therefore of something like forgetfulness, exist in the Absolute Mind. I presume that only God's attention keeps me (or anything else) in existence at all.

What, then, are we really doing? Our whole conception of, so to call it, the prayer-situation depends on the answer.

We are always completely, and therefore equally, known to God. That is our destiny whether we like it or not. But though this knowledge never varies, the quality of our being known can. A school of thought holds that "freedom is willed necessity." Never mind if they are right or not. I want this idea only as an analogy. Ordinarily, to be known by God is to be, for this purpose, in the category of things. We are like earthworms, cabbages, and nebulae, objects of divine knowledge. But when we (a) become aware of the fact—the present fact, not the generalisation—and (b) assent with all our will to be so known, then we treat ourselves, in relation to God, not as things but as persons. We have unveiled. Not that any veil could have baffled this sight. The change is in us. The passive changes to the active. Instead of merely being known, we show, we tell, we offer ourselves to view.

To put ourselves thus on a personal footing with God could, in itself and without warrant, be nothing but presumption and illusion. But we are taught that it is not; that it is God who gives us that footing. For it is by the Holy Spirit that we cry "Father." By unveiling, by confessing our sins and "making known" our requests, we assume the high rank of persons before Him. And He, descending, becomes a Person to us.

But I should not have said "becomes." In Him there is no becoming. He reveals Himself as Person: or reveals that in Him which is Person. For—dare one say it? in a book it would need pages of qualification and insurance—God is in some measure to a man as that man is to God. The door in God that opens is the door he knocks at. (At least, I think so, usually.) The Person in Him—He is more than a person —meets those who can welcome or at least face it. He speaks as "I" when we truly call Him "Thou." (How good Buber is!)

This talk of "meeting" is, no doubt, anthropomorphic; as if God and I could be face to face, like two fellow-creatures, when in reality He is above me and within me and below me and all about me. That is why it must be balanced by all manner of metaphysical and theological abstractions. But never, here or anywhere else, let us think that while anthropomorphic images are a concession to our weakness, the abstractions are the literal truth. Both are equally concessions; each singly misleading, and the two together mutually corrective. Unless you sit to it very tightly, continually mur-

muring "Not thus, not thus, neither is this Thou," the abstraction is fatal. It will make the life of lives inanimate and the love of loves impersonal. The *naïf* image is mischievous chiefly in so far as it holds unbelievers back from conversion. It does believers, even at its crudest, no harm. What soul ever perished for believing that God the Father really has a beard?

Your other question is one which, I think, really gets in pious people's way. It was, you remember, "How important must a need or desire be before we can properly make it the subject of a petition?" *Properly,* I take it, here means either "without irreverence" or "without silliness," or both.

When I'd thought about it for a bit, it seemed to me that there are really two questions involved.

1. How important must an object be before we can, without sin and folly, allow our desire for it to become a matter of serious concern to us? This, you see, is a question about what old writers call our "frame"; that is, our "frame of mind."

2. Granted the existence of such a serious concern in our minds, can it always be properly laid before God in prayer?

We all know the answer to the first of these in theory. We must aim at what St. Augustine (is it?) calls "ordinate loves." Our deepest concern should be for first things, and our next deepest for second things, and so on down to zero—to total absence of concern for things that are not really good, nor means to good, at all.

Meantime, however, we want to know not how we should pray if we were perfect but how we should pray being as we now are. And if my idea of prayer as "unveiling" is accepted, we have already answered this. It is no use to ask God with factitious earnestness for A when our whole mind is in reality filled with the desire for B. We must lay before Him what is in us, not what ought to be in us.

22

Even an intimate human friend is ill-used if we talk to him about one thing while our mind is really on another, and even a human friend will soon become aware when we are doing so. You yourself came to see me a few years ago when the great blow had fallen upon me. I tried to talk to you as if nothing were wrong. You saw through it in five minutes. Then I confessed. And you said things which made me ashamed of my attempt at concealment.

It may well be that the desire can be laid before God only as a sin to be repented; but one of the best ways of learning this is to lay it before God. Your problem, however, was not about sinful desires in that sense; rather, about desires, intrinsically innocent and sinning, if at all, only by being stronger than the triviality of their object warrants. I have no doubt at all that if they are the subject of our thoughts they must be the subject of our prayers—whether in penitence or in petition or in a little of both: penitence for the excess, yet petition for the thing we desire.

If one forcibly excludes them, don't they wreck all the rest of our prayers? If we lay all the cards on the table, God will help us to moderate the excesses. But the pressure of things we are trying to keep out of our mind is a hopeless distraction. As someone said, "No noise is so emphatic as one you are trying not to listen to."

The ordinate frame of mind is one of the blessings we must pray for, not a fancy-dress we must put on when we pray.

And perhaps, as those who do not turn to God in petty trials will have no *habit* or such resort to help them when the great trials come, so those who have not learned to ask Him for childish things will have less readiness to ask Him for great ones. We must not be too high-minded. I fancy we may sometimes be deterred from small prayers by a sense of our own dignity rather than of God's.

V

I DON'T very much like the job of telling you "more about my festoonings"—the private overtones I give to certain petitions. I make two conditions: 1) That you will in return tell me some of yours. 2) That you will understand I am not in the least *recommending* mine either to you or to anyone else. There could be many better; and my present festoons will very probably change.

I call them "festoons," by the way, because they don't (I trust) obliterate the plain, public sense of the petition but are merely hung on it.

What I do about "hallowed be thy name" I told you a fortnight ago.

Thy kingdom come. That is, may your reign be realised here, as it is realised there. But I tend to take *there* on three levels. First, as in the sinless world beyond the horrors of animal and human life; in the behaviour of stars and trees and water, in sunrise and wind. May there be *here* (in my heart) the beginning of a like beauty. Secondly, as in the best human lives I have known: in all the people who really bear the burdens and ring true, and in the quiet, busy, ordered life of really good families and really good religious houses. May that too be "here." Finally, of course, in the usual sense: as in Heaven, as among the blessed dead.

And *here* can of course be taken not only as "in my heart," but as "in this college"—in England—in the world in general. But prayer is not the time for pressing our own favourite social or political panacea. Even Queen Victoria didn't like "being talked to as if she were a public meeting."

Thy will be done. My festoons on this have been added gradually. At first I took it exclusively as an act of submission, attempting to do with it what Our Lord did in Gethsemane. I thought of God's will purely as something that would come upon me, something of which I should be the patient. And I also thought of it as a will which would be embodied in pains and disappointments. Not, to be sure, that I supposed God's will for me to consist entirely of disagreeables. But I thought it was only the disagreeables that called for this preliminary submission—the agreeables could look after themselves for the present. When they turned up, one could give thanks.

This interpretation is, I expect, the commonest. And so it must be. And such are the miseries of human life that it must often fill our whole mind. But at other times other meanings can be added. So I added one more.

The peg for it is, I admit, much more obvious in the English version than in the Greek or Latin. No matter: this is where the liberty of festooning comes in. "Thy will *be done*." But a great deal of it is to be done by God's creatures;

including me. The petition, then, is not merely that I may patiently suffer God's will but also that I may vigorously do it. I must be an agent as well as a patient. I am asking that I may be enabled to do it. In the long run I am asking to be given "the same mind which was also in Christ."

Taken this way, I find the words have a more regular daily application. For there isn't always—or we don't always have reason to suspect that there is—some great affliction looming in the near future, but there are always duties to be done; usually, for me, neglected duties to be caught up with. "Thy will be *done*—by me—now" brings one back to brass tacks.

But more than that, I am at this very moment contemplating a new festoon. Tell me if you think it a vain subtlety. I am beginning to feel that we need a preliminary act of submission not only towards possible future afflictions but also towards possible future blessings. I know it sounds fantastic; but think it over. It seems to me that we often, almost sulkily, reject the good that God offers us because, at that moment, we expected some other good. Do you know what I mean? On every level of our life—in our religious experience, in our gastronomic, erotic, aesthetic, and social experience—we are always harking back to some occasion which seemed to us to reach perfection, setting that up as a norm, and depreciating all other occasions by comparison. But these other occasions, I now suspect, are often full of their own new blessing, if only we would lay ourselves open to it. God shows us a new facet of the glory, and we refuse to look at it because we're still looking for the old one. And of course we don't get that. You can't, at the twentieth reading, get again the experience of reading *Lycidas* for the first time. But what you do get can be in its own way as good.

This applies especially to the devotional life. Many religious people lament that the first fervours of their conversion have died away. They think—sometimes rightly, but not, I believe, always—that their sins account for this. They may even try by pitiful efforts of will to revive what now seem to have been the golden days. But were those fervours —the operative word is *those*—ever intended to last?

It would be rash to say that there is any prayer which God *never* grants. But the strongest candidate is the prayer we might express in the single word *encore*. And how should the Infinite repeat Himself? All space and time are too little for Him to utter Himself in them *once*.

And the joke, or tragedy, of it all is that these golden moments in the past, which are so tormenting if we erect them into a norm, are entirely nourishing, wholesome, and enchanting if we are content to accept them for what they are, for memories. Properly bedded down in a past which we do not miserably try to conjure back, they will send up exquisite growths. Leave the bulbs alone, and the new flowers will come up. Grub them up and hope, by fondling and sniffing, to get last year's blooms, and you will get nothing. "Unless a seed die . . ."

I expect we all do much the same with the prayer for *our daily bread*. It means, doesn't it, all we need for the day— "things requisite and necessary as well for the body as for the soul." I should hate to make this clause "purely religious" by thinking of "spiritual" needs alone. One of its uses, to me, is to remind us daily that what Burnaby calls the *naïf* view of prayer is firmly built into Our Lord's teaching.

Forgive us . . . as we forgive. Unfortunately there's no need to do any festooning here. To forgive for the moment is not difficult. But to go on forgiving, to forgive the same offence again every time it recurs to the memory—there's the real tussle. My resource is to look for some action of my own which is open to the same charge as the one I'm resenting. If I still smart to remember how A let me down, I must

27

still remember how I let B down. If I find it difficult to forgive those who bullied me at school, let me, at that very moment, remember, and pray for, those I bullied. (Not that we called it *bullying*, of course. That is where prayer without words can be so useful. In it there are no names; therefore no *aliases*.)

I was never worried myself by the words *lead us not into temptation,* but a great many of my correspondents are. The words suggest to them what someone has called "a fiend-like conception of God," as one who first forbids us certain fruits and then lures us to taste them. But the Greek word (πειρασμός) means "trial"—"trying circumstances"—of every sort; a far larger word than English "temptation." So that the petition essentially is "Make straight our paths. Spare us, where possible, from all crises, whether of temptation or affliction." By the way, you yourself, though you've doubtless forgotten it, gave me an excellent gloss on it: years ago in the pub at Coton. You said it added a sort of reservation to all our preceding prayers. As if we said, "In my ignorance I have asked for A, B, and C. But don't give me them if you foresee that they would in reality be to me either snares or sorrows." And you quoted Juvenal, *numinibus vota exaudita malignis,* "enormous prayers which heaven in vengeance grants." For we make plenty of such prayers. If God had granted all the silly prayers I've made in my life, where should I be now?

I don't often use *the kingdom, the power, and the glory.* When I do, I have an idea of the *kingdom* as sovereignty *de jure;* God, as good, would have a claim on my obedience even if He had no power. The *power* is the sovereignty *de facto*—He is omnipotent. And the *glory* is—well, the glory; the "beauty so old and new," the "light from behind the sun."

VI

I CAN'T remember exactly what I said about not making the petition for our daily bread too "religious," and I'm not quite sure what you mean—nor how ironically—by asking if I've become "one of Vidler's young men"!

About Vidler. I never heard the programme which created all that scandal, and naturally one wouldn't condemn a dog on newspaper extracts. But I have now read his essay in *Soundings* and I believe I go a good deal further with him than you would. Much of what he quotes from F. D. Maurice and Bonhoeffer seems to me very good; and so, I think, are his own arguments for the Establishment.

At any rate I can well understand how a man who is trying to love God and his neighbour should come to dislike the very word *religion;* a word, by the way, which hardly ever appears in the New Testament. Newman makes my blood run cold when he says in one of the *Parochial and Plain Sermons* that Heaven is like a church because, in both, "one single sovereign subject—religion—is brought before us." He forgets that there is no temple in the new Jerusalem.

He has substituted *religion* for God—as if navigation were substituted for arrival, or battle for victory, or wooing for marriage, or in general the means for the end. But even in this present life, there is danger in the very concept of *religion.* It carries the suggestion that this is one more department of life, an extra department added to the economic, the social, the intellectual, the recreational, and all the rest. But that whose claims are infinite can have no standing as a department. Either it is an illusion or else our whole life falls under it. We have no non-religious activities; only religious and irreligious.

Religion, nevertheless, appears to exist as a department, and, in some ages, to thrive as such. It thrives partly because there exists in many people a "love of religious observances," which I think Simone Weil is quite right in regarding as a merely natural taste. There exists also—Vidler is rather good on this—the delight in religious (as in any other) organisation. Then all sorts of aesthetic, sentimental, historical, political interests are drawn in. Finally sales of work, the parish magazine, and bell-ringing, and Santa Claus.

None of them bad things. But none of them is necessarily of more spiritual value than the activities we call secular. And they are infinitely dangerous when this is not understood. This department of life, labelled "sacred," can become an end in itself; an idol that hides both God and my neighbours. ("When the means are autonomous they are deadly.") It may even come about that a man's most genuinely Christian actions fall entirely outside that part of his life which he calls *religious*.

I read in a religious paper, "Nothing is more important than to teach children to use the sign of the cross." Nothing? Not compassion, nor veracity, nor justice? *Voilà l'ennemi.*

One must, however, walk warily, for the truth that *religion* as a department has really no right to exist can be misunderstood. Some will conclude that this illegitimate department ought to be abolished. Others will think, coming nearer to the truth, that it ought to cease to be departmental by being extended to the whole of life, but will misinterpret this. They will think it means that more and more of our secular transactions should be "opened with prayer," that a wearisomely explicit pietism should infest our talk, that there should be no more cakes and ale. A third sort, well aware that God still rules a very small part of their lives, and that "a departmental religion" is no good, may despair. It would have to be carefully explained to them to be "still only a part" is not the same as being a permanent department. In all of us God "still" holds only a part. D-Day is only a week ago. The bite so far taken out of Normandy shows small on the map of Europe. The resistance is strong, the casualties heavy, and the event uncertain. There is, we have to admit, a line of demarcation between God's part in us and the enemy's region. But it is, we hope, a fighting line; not a frontier fixed by agreement.

But I suspect the real misunderstanding of Vidler's talk lay elsewhere. We have been speaking of *religion* as a pattern of behaviour—which, if contentedly departmental, cannot really be Christian behaviour. But people also, and more often, use *religion* to mean a system of beliefs. When they heard that Vidler wanted a church with "less religion," they thought he meant that the little—the very little—which

31

liberal theology has still left of the "faith once given" was to be emptied out. Hence someone asked, "Is he a Theist?"

Well, he certainly is. He wants—I think he wants very earnestly—to retain some Christian doctrines. But he is prepared to scrap a good deal. "Traditional doctrines" are to be tested. Many things will have to be "outgrown" or "survive chiefly as venerable archaisms or as fairy-stories." He feels quite happy about this undefined programme of jettison because he trusts in the continued guidance of the Holy Spirit. A noble faith; provided, of course, there is any such being as the Holy Spirit. But I suppose His existence is itself one of the "traditional doctrines" which, on Vidler's premises, we might any day find we had outgrown. So with the doctrine— Vidler calls it "the fact"—that man is "a two-fold creature— not only a political creature, but also a spiritual being." Vidler and you and I (and Plato) think it a fact. Tens of thousands, perhaps millions, think it a fantasy. The neutral description of it is "a traditional doctrine." Do you think he means that these two doctrines—and why just these two?— are the hard core of his belief, exempt from the threat of rejection which overhangs all other doctrines? Or would he say that, as the title of the book implies, he is only "taking soundings"—and if the line is not long enough to reach bottom, soundings can yield only negative information to the navigator?

I was interested in the things you said about *forgive us our trespasses*. Often, to be sure, there is something definite for which to ask forgiveness. This is plain sailing. But, like you, I often find one or other of two less manageable states: either a vague feeling of guilt or a sly, and equally vague, self-approval. What are we to do with these?

Many modern psychologists tell us always to distrust this vague feeling of guilt, as something purely pathological. And if they had stopped at that, I might believe them. But when they go on, as some do, to apply the same treatment to all guilt-feelings whatever, to suggest that one's feeling about a particular unkind act or a particular insincerity is also and equally untrustworthy—I can't help thinking they are talking nonsense. One sees this the moment one looks at other people. I have talked to some who felt guilt when they jolly well ought to have felt it; they have behaved like brutes and know it. I've also met others who felt guilty and weren't guilty by any standard I can apply. And thirdly, I've met people who were guilty and didn't seem to feel guilt. And isn't this what we should expect? People can be *malades imaginaires* who are well and think they are ill; and others, especially consumptives, are ill and think they are well; and thirdly—far the largest class—people are ill and know they are ill. It would be very odd if there were any region in which all mistakes were in one direction.

Some Christians would tell us to go on rummaging and scratching till we find something specific. We may be sure, they say, that there are real sins enough to justify the guilt-feeling or to overthrow the feeling that all is well. I think they are right in saying that if we hunt long enough we shall find, or think we have found, something. But that is just what wakens suspicion. A theory which could never by any experience be falsified can for that reason hardly be verified. And just as, when we are yielding to temptation, we make ourselves believe that what we have always thought a sin will on this occasion, for some strange reason, not be a sin, shan't we persuade ourselves that something we have always (rightly) thought to be innocent was really wrong? We may create scruples. And scruples are always a bad thing—if only because they usually distract us from real duties.

I don't at all know whether I'm right or not, but I have, on the whole, come to the conclusion that one can't directly *do* anything about either feeling. One is not to believe either—indeed, how can one believe a fog? I come back to St. John: "if our heart condemn us, God is greater than our heart." And equally, if our heart flatter us, God is greater than our heart. I sometimes pray not for self-knowledge in general but for just so much self-knowledge at the moment as I can bear and use at the moment; the little daily dose.

Have we any reason to suppose that total self-knowledge, if it were given us, would be for our good? Children and fools, we are told, should never look at half-done work; and we are not yet, I trust, even half-done. You and I wouldn't, at all stages, think it wise to tell a pupil exactly what we thought of his quality. It is much more important that he should know what to do next.

If one said this in public one would have all the Freudians on one's back. And, mind you, we are greatly indebted to them. They did expose the cowardly evasions of really useful self-knowledge which we had all been practising from the beginning of the world. But there is also a merely morbid and fidgety curiosity about one's self—the slop-over from modern psychology—which surely does no good? The unfinished picture would so like to jump off the easel and have a look at itself! And analysis doesn't cure that. We all know people who have undergone it and seem to have made themselves a lifelong subject of research ever since.

If I am right, the conclusion is that when our conscience won't come down to brass-tacks but will only vaguely accuse or vaguely approve, we must say to it, like Herbert, "Peace, prattler"—and get on.

VII

Iᶠ you meant in your last letter that we can scrap the whole idea of petitionary prayer—prayer which, as you put it, calls upon God to "engineer" particular events in the objective world—and confine ourselves to acts of penitence and adoration, I disagree with you. It may be true that Christianity would be, intellectually, a far easier religion if it told us to do this. And I can understand the people who think it would also be a more high-minded religion. But remember the psalm: "Lord, I am not high minded." Or better still, remember the New Testament. The most unblushingly petitionary prayers are there recommended to us both by precept and example. Our Lord in Gethsemane made a petitionary prayer (and did not get what He asked for).

You'll remind me that He asked with a reservation—"nevertheless, not my will but thine." This makes an enormous difference. But the difference which it precisely does not make is that of removing the prayer's petitionary character. When poor Bill, on a famous occasion, asked us to advance him £100, he said, "If you are sure you can spare it," and "I shall quite understand if you'd rather not." This made his request very different from the nagging or even threatening request which a different sort of man might have made. But it was still a request.

The servant is not greater, and must not be more high-minded, than the master. Whatever the theoretical difficulties are, we must continue to make requests of God. And on this point we can get no help from those who keep on reminding us that this is the lowest and least essential kind of prayer. They may be right; but so what? Diamonds are more precious than cairngorms, but the cairngorms still exist and must be taken into account like anything else.

But don't let us be too easily brow-beaten. Some of the popular objections to petitionary prayer, if they are valid against it, are equally valid against other things which we all do whether we are Christians or not, and have done ever since the world began, and shall certainly continue to do. I don't think the burden of answering these rests especially on us.

There is, for example, the Determinism which, whether under that name or another, seems to be implicit in a scientific view of the world. Determinism does not deny the existence of human behaviour. It rejects as an illusion our spontaneous conviction that our behaviour has its ultimate origin in ourselves. What I call "my act" is the conduit-pipe through which the torrent of the universal process passes, and was bound to pass, at a particular time and place. The distinction between what we call the "voluntary" and the "involuntary" movements of our own bodies is not obliterated, but turns out (on this view) to be not exactly the sort of difference we supposed. What I call the "involuntary" movements necessarily—and, if we know enough, predictably—result from mechanical causes outside my body or from pathological or organic processes within it. The "voluntary" ones result from conscious psychological factors which themselves result from unconscious psychological factors dependent on my economic situation, my infantile and pre-natal experience, my heredity . . . and so on back to the beginnings of organic life and beyond. I am a conductor, not a source. I never make an original contribution to the world-process. I move with that process not even as a floating log moves with the river but as a particular pint of the water itself moves.

But even those who believe this will, like anyone else, ask you to hand them the salt. Every form of behaviour, including speech, can go on just the same, and will. If a strict determinist believed in God (and I think he might) petitionary prayer would be no more irrational in him than in anyone else.

Another argument, put up (but not accepted) by Burnaby in *Soundings,* is this. If man's freedom is to be of any value, if he is to have any power of planning and of adapting means to ends, he must live in a predictable world. But if God alters the course of events in answer to prayer, then the world will be unpredictable. Therefore, if man is to be effectively free, God must be in this respect un-free.

But is it not plain that this predictable world, whether it is necessary to our freedom or no, is not the world we live in? This is a world of bets and insurance policies, of hopes and anxieties, where "nothing is certain but the unexpected" and prudence lies in "the masterly administration of the unforeseen." Nearly all the things people pray about are unpredictable: the result of a battle or an operation, the losing or getting of a job, the reciprocation of a love. We don't pray about eclipses.

But, you will reply, we once did. Every advance of science makes predictable something that was formerly unpredictable. It is only our ignorance that makes petitionary prayer possible. Would it not be rational to assume that all those events we now pray about are in principle just as predictable —though we don't yet know enough to predict them—as things like eclipses? But that is no answer to the point I'm making. I am not now trying to refute Determinism. I am only arguing that a world where the future is unknown cannot be inconsistent with planned and purposive action since we are actually planning and purposing in such a world now and have been doing so for thousands of years.

Also, between ourselves, I think this objection involves a false idea of what the sciences do. You are here a better judge than I, but I give it for what it may be worth. It is true in one sense that the mark of a genuine science is its power to predict. But does this mean that a perfected science, or a perfected synthesis of all the sciences, would be able to write reliable histories of the future? And would the scientists even want to do so? Doesn't science predict a future event only in so far as, and only because, that event is the instance of some universal law? Everything that makes the event unique—in other words, everything that makes it a concrete historical event—is deliberately ruled out; not only as something which science can't, or can't yet, include, but also as something in which science, as such, has no interest. No one sunrise has ever been exactly like another. Take away from the sunrises that in which they differ and what is left will be identical. Such abstracted identicals are what science predicts. But life as we live it is not reducible to such identities. Every real physical event, much more every human experience, has behind it, in the long run, the whole previous history of the real universe—which is not itself an "instance" of anything—and is therefore always festooned with those particularities which science for her own purposes quite rightly discounts. Doesn't the whole art of contriving a good experiment consist in devising means whereby the irrelevancies—that is, the historical particularities—can be reduced to the minimum?

Later in his essay Burnaby seems to suggest that human wills are the only radically unpredictable factor in history. I'm not happy about this. Partly because I don't see how the gigantic negative which it involves could be proved; partly because I agree with Bradley that unpredictability is not the essence, nor even a symptom, of freedom. (Did you see they've reprinted *Ethical Studies*? The baiting of Arnold, wholly just and in Arnold's own manner, is exquisite.) But suppose it were true. Even then, it would make such a huge rent in the predictability of events that the whole idea of predictability as somehow necessary to human life would be in ruins. Think of the countless human acts, acts of copulation, spread over millennia, that led to the birth of Plato, Attila, or Napoleon. Yet it is on these unpredictables that human history largely depends. Twenty-five years ago you asked Betty to marry you. And now, as a result, we have young George (I hope he's got over his gastric flu?). A thousand years hence he might have a good many descendants, and only modesty could conceal from you the possibility that one of these might have as huge a historical effect as Aristotle—or Hitler!

VIII

W_{HAT} froth and bubble my last letter must have seemed to you! I had hardly posted it when I got Betty's card with the disquieting news about George—turning my jocular reference to his descendants into a stab (at least I suppose it did) and making our whole discussion on prayer seem to you, as it now does to me, utterly unreal. The distance between the abstract "Does God hear petitionary prayers?" and the concrete "Will He—can He—grant our prayers for George?" is apparently infinite.

Not of course that I can pretend for a moment to be able to feel it as you do. If I did, you would say to yourself (like the man in *Macbeth*), "He has no children." A few years ago when I was in my own trouble you said as much to me. You wrote, "I know I'm outside. My voice can hardly reach you." And that was one reason why your letter was more like the real grasp of a real hand than any other I got.

The temptation is to attempt reassurances: to remind you how often a G.P.'s preliminary diagnosis is wrong, that the symptoms are admittedly ambiguous, that threatened men sometimes live to a ripe old age. And it would all in fact be true. But what, in that way, could I say which you are not saying to yourself every hour? And you would know my motive. You'd know how little real scientific candour—or knowledge—lay behind my words. And if, which God forbid, your suspense ended as terribly as mine did, these reassurances would sound like mockeries. So at least I found. The memory of the false hopes was an additional torment. Even now certain remembered moments of fallacious comfort twist my heart more than the remembered moment of despair.

All may yet be well. This is true. Meanwhile you have the waiting—waiting till the X rays are developed and till the specialist has completed his observations. And while you wait, you still have to go on living—if only one could go underground, hibernate, sleep it out. And then (for me—I believe you are stronger) the horrible by-products of anxiety; the incessant, circular movement of the thoughts, even the Pagan temptation to keep watch for irrational omens. And one prays; but mainly such prayers as are themselves a form of anguish.

Some people feel guilty about their anxieties and regard them as a defect of faith. I don't agree at all. They are afflictions, not sins. Like all afflictions, they are, if we can so take them, our share in the Passion of Christ. For the beginning of the Passion—the first move, so to speak—is in Geth-semane. In Gethsemane a very strange and significant thing seems to have happened.

It is clear from many of His sayings that Our Lord had long foreseen His death. He knew what conduct such as His, in a world such as we have made of this, must inevitably lead to. But it is clear that this knowledge must somehow have been withdrawn from Him before He prayed in Geth-semane. He could not, with whatever reservation about the Father's will, have prayed that the cup might pass and simul-taneously known that it would not. That is both a logical and a psychological impossibility. You see what this involves? Lest any trial incident to humanity should be lacking, the torments of hope—of suspense, anxiety—were at the last moment loosed upon Him—the supposed possibility that, after all, He might, He just conceivably might, be spared the supreme horror. There was precedent. Isaac had been spared: he too at the last moment, he also against all ap-parent probability. It was not quite impossible . . . and doubtless He had seen other men crucified . . . a sight very unlike most of our religious pictures and images.

But for this last (and erroneous) hope against hope, and the consequent tumult of the soul, the sweat of blood, per-haps He would not have been very Man. To live in a fully predictable world is not to be a man.

At the end, I know, we are told that an angel appeared "comforting" Him. But neither *comforting* in sixteenth-cen-tury English nor ἐννισχύων in Greek means "consoling." "Strengthening" is more the word. May not the strengthen-ing have consisted in the renewed certainty—cold comfort this—that the thing must be endured and therefore could be?

We all try to accept with some sort of submission our

afflictions when they actually arrive. But the prayer in Gethsemane shows that the preceding anxiety is equally God's will and equally part of our human destiny. The perfect Man experienced it. And the servant is not greater than the master. We are Christians, not Stoics.

Does not every movement in the Passion write large some common element in the sufferings of our race? First, the prayer of anguish; not granted. Then He turns to His friends. They are asleep—as ours, or we, are so often, or busy, or away, or preoccupied. Then He faces the Church; the very Church that He brought into existence. It condemns Him. This also is characteristic. In every Church, in every institution, there is something which sooner or later works against the very purpose for which it came into existence. But there seems to be another chance. There is the State; in this case, the Roman state. Its pretensions are far lower than those of the Jewish church, but for that very reason it may be free from local fanaticisms. It claims to be just on a rough, worldly level. Yes, but only so far as is consistent with political expediency and *raison d'état*. One becomes a counter in a complicated game. But even now all is not lost. There is still an appeal to the People—the poor and simple whom He had blessed, whom He had healed and fed and taught, to whom He Himself belongs. But they have become over-night (it is nothing unusual) a murderous rabble shouting for His blood. There is, then, nothing left but God. And to God, God's last words are "Why hast thou forsaken me?"

You see how characteristic, how representative, it all is. The human situation writ large. These are among the things it means to be a man. Every rope breaks when you seize it. Every door is slammed shut as you reach it. To be like the fox at the end of the run; the earths all staked.

As for the last dereliction of all, how can we either understand or endure it? Is it that God Himself cannot be Man unless God seems to vanish at His greatest need? And if so, why? I sometimes wonder if we have even begun to understand what is involved in the very concept of creation. If God will create, He will make something to be, and yet to be not Himself. To be created is, in some sense, to be ejected or separated. Can it be that the more perfect the creature is, the further this separation must at some point be pushed? It is saints, not common people, who experience the "dark night." It is men and angels, not beasts, who rebel. Inanimate matter sleeps in the bosom of the Father. The "hiddenness" of God perhaps presses most painfully on those who are in another way nearest to Him, and therefore God Himself, made man, will of all men be by God most forsaken? One of the seventeenth-century divines says, "By pretending to be visible God could only deceive the world." Perhaps He does pretend just a little to simple souls who need a full measure of "sensible consolation." Not deceiving them, but tempering the wind to the shorn lamb. Of course I'm not saying like Niebuhr that evil is inherent in finitude. That would identify the creation with the fall and make God the author of evil. But perhaps there is an anguish, an alienation, a crucifixion involved in the creative act. Yet He who alone can judge judges the far-off consummation to be worth it.

I am, you see, a Job's comforter. Far from lightening the dark valley where you now find yourself, I blacken it. And you know why. Your darkness has brought back my own. But on second thoughts I don't regret what I have written. I think it is only in a shared darkness that you and I can really meet at present; shared with one another and, what matters most, with our Master. We are not on an untrodden path. Rather, on the main-road.

Certainly we were talking too lightly and easily about these things a fortnight ago. We were playing with counters. One used to be told as a child: "Think what you're saying." Apparently we need also to be told: "Think what you're thinking." The stakes have to be raised before we take the game quite seriously. I know this is the opposite of what is often said about the necessity of keeping all emotion out of our intellectual processes—"you can't think straight unless you are cool." But then neither can you think deep if you are. I suppose one must try every problem in both states. You remember that the ancient Persians debated everything twice: once when they were drunk and once when they were sober.

I know one of you will let me have news as soon as there is any.

IX

THANK God. What a mare's nest! Or, more grimly, what a rehearsal! It is only twenty-four hours since I got Betty's wire, and already the crisis seems curiously far away. Like at sea. Once you have doubled the point and got into smooth water, the point doesn't take long to hide below the horizon.

And now, your letter. I'm not at all surprised at your feeling flattened rather than joyful. That isn't ingratitude. It's only exhaustion. Weren't there moments even during those terrible days when you glided into a sort of apathy—for the same reason? The body (bless it) will not continue indefinitely supplying us with the physical media of emotion.

Surely there's no difficulty about the prayer in Gethsemane on the ground that if the disciples were asleep they couldn't have heard it and therefore couldn't have recorded it? The words they did record would hardly have taken three seconds to utter. He was only "a stone's throw" away. The silence of night was around them. And we may be sure He prayed aloud. People did everything aloud in those days. You remember how astonished St. Augustine was—some centuries later in a far more sophisticated society—to discover that when St. Ambrose was reading (to himself) you couldn't hear the words even if you went and stood just beside him? The disciples heard the opening words of the prayer before they went to sleep. They record those opening words as if they were the whole.

There is a rather amusing instance of the same thing in Acts XXIV. The Jews had got down a professional orator called Tertullos to conduct the prosecution of St. Paul. The speech as recorded by St. Luke takes eighty-four words in the Greek, if I've counted correctly. Eighty-four words are impossibly short for a Greek advocate on a full-dress occasion. Presumably, then, they are a *précis?* But of those eighty-odd words forty are taken up with preliminary compliments to the bench—stuff which, in a *précis* on that tiny scale, ought not to have come in at all. It is easy to guess what has happened. St. Luke, though an excellent narrator, was no good as a reporter. He starts off by trying to memorise, or to get down, the whole speech *verbatim.* And he succeeds in reproducing a certain amount of the exordium (the style unmistakable. Only a practising *rhetor* ever talks that way). But he is soon defeated. The whole of the rest of the speech has to be represented by a ludicrously inadequate abstract. But he doesn't tell us what has happened, and thus seems to attribute to Tertullos a performance which would have spelled professional ruin.

As you say, the problems about prayer which really press upon a man when he is praying for dear life are not the general and philosophical ones; they are those that arise within Christianity itself. At least, this is so for you and me. We have long since agreed that if our prayers are granted at all they are granted from the foundation of the world. God and His acts are not in time. Intercourse between God and man occurs at particular moments for the man, but not for God. If there is—as the very concept of prayer presupposes—an adaptation between the free actions of men in prayer and the course of events, this adaptation is from the beginning inherent in the great single creative act. Our prayers are heard —don't say "have been heard" or you are putting God into time—not only before we make them but before we are made ourselves.

The real problems are different. Is it our faith that prayers, or some prayers, are real causes? But they are not magical causes: they don't, like spells, act directly on nature. They act, then, on nature through God? This would seem to imply that they act on God. But God, we believe, is impassible. All theology would reject the idea of a transaction in which a creature was the agent and God the patient.

It is quite useless to try to answer this empirically by producing stories—though you and I could tell strange ones— of striking answers to prayer. We shall be told, reasonably enough, that *post hoc* is not *propter hoc*. The thing we prayed for was going to happen anyway. Our action was irrelevant. Even a fellow-creature's action which fulfils our request may not be caused by it; he does what we ask, but perhaps he would equally have done so without our asking. Some cynics will tell us that no woman ever married a man *because* he proposed to her: she always elicits the proposal because she has determined to marry him.

In these human instances we believe, when we do believe, that our request was the cause, or *a* cause, of the other party's action, because we have from deep acquaintance a certain impression of that party's character. Certainly not by applying the scientific procedures—control experiments, etc. —for establishing causes. Similarly we believe, when we do believe, that the relation between our prayer and the event is not a mere coincidence only because we have a certain idea of God's character. Only faith vouches for the connection. No empirical proof could establish it. Even a miracle, if one occurred, "might have been going to happen anyway."

Again, in the most intimate human instances we really feel that the category of cause and effect will not contain what actually happens. In a real "proposal"—as distinct from one in an old-fashioned novel—is there any agent-patient relation? Which drop on the window pane moves to join the other?

Now I am going to suggest that strictly causal thinking is even more inadequate when applied to the relation between God and man. I don't mean only when we are thinking of prayer, but whenever we are thinking about what happens at the Frontier, at the mysterious point of junction and separation where absolute being utters derivative being.

One attempt to define causally what happens there has led to the whole puzzle about grace and free will. You will notice that Scripture just sails over the problem. "Work out your own salvation in fear and trembling"—pure Pelagianism. But why? "For it is God who worketh in you"—pure Augustinianism. It is presumably only our presuppositions that make this appear nonsensical. We profanely assume that divine and human action exclude one another like the actions of two fellow-creatures so that "God did this" and "I did this" cannot both be true of the same act except in the sense that each contributed a share.

In the end we must admit a two-way traffic at the junction. At first sight no passive verb in the world would seem to be so utterly passive as "to be created." Does it not mean "to *have been* nonentity"? Yet, for us rational creatures, to be created also means "to be made agents." We have nothing that we have not received; but part of what we have received is the power of being something more than receptacles. We exercise it, no doubt, chiefly by our sins. But they, for my present argument, will do as well as anything else. For God forgives sins. He would not do so if we committed none—"whereto serves Mercy but to confront the visage of offence?" In that sense the divine action is consequent upon, conditioned by, elicited by, our behaviour. Does this mean that we can "act upon" God? I suppose you could put it that way if you wanted. If you do, then we must interpret His "impassibility" in a way which admits this; for we know that God forgives much better than we know what "impassible" means. I would rather say that from before all worlds His providential and creative act (for they are all one) takes into account all the situations produced by the acts of His creatures. And if He takes our sins into account, why not our petitions?

X

I SEE your point. But you must admit that Scripture doesn't take the slightest pains to guard the doctrine of Divine Impassibility. We are constantly represented as exciting the Divine wrath or pity—even as "grieving" God. I know this language is analogical. But when we say that, we must not smuggle in the idea that we can throw the analogy away and, as it were, get in behind it to a purely literal truth. All we can really substitute for the analogical expression is some theological abstraction. And the abstraction's value is almost entirely negative. It warns us against drawing absurd consequences from the analogical expression by prosaic extrapolations. By itself, the abstraction "impassible" can get us nowhere. It might even suggest something far more misleading than the most *naïf* Old Testament picture of a stormily emotional Jehovah. Either something inert, or something which was "Pure Act" in such a sense that it could take no account of events within the universe it had created.

I suggest two rules for exegetics: 1) Never take the images literally. 2) When the *purport* of the images—what they say to our fear and hope and will and affections—seems to conflict with the theological abstractions, trust the purport of the images every time. For our abstract thinking is itself a tissue of analogies: a continual modelling of spiritual reality in legal or chemical or mechanical terms. Are these likely to be more adequate than the sensuous, organic, and personal images of Scripture—light and darkness, river and well, seed and harvest, master and servant, hen and chickens, father and child? The footprints of the Divine are more visible in that rich soil than across rocks or slag-heaps. Hence what they now call "demythologising" Christianity can easily be "re-mythologising" it—and substituting a poorer mythology for a richer.

I agree that my deliberately vague expression about our prayers being "taken into account" is a retreat from Pascal's magnificent dictum ("God has instituted prayer so as to confer upon His creatures the dignity of being causes"). But Pascal really does suggest a far too explicit agent-and-patient relation, with God as the patient. And I have another ground for preferring my own more modest formula. To think of our prayers as just "causes" would suggest that the whole importance of petitionary prayer lay in the achievement of the thing asked for. But really, for our spiritual life as a whole, the "being taken into account," or "considered," matters more than the being granted. Religious people don't talk about the "results" of prayer; they talk of its being "an-

swered" or "heard." Someone said, "A suitor wants his suit
to be heard as well as granted." In suits to God, if they are
really religious acts at all and not merely attempts at magic,
this is even more so. We can bear to be refused but not to
be ignored. In other words, our faith can survive many
refusals if they really are refusals and not mere disregards.
The apparent stone will be bread to us if we believe that a
Father's hand put it into ours, in mercy or in justice or even
in rebuke. It is hard and bitter, yet it can be chewed and
swallowed. But if, having prayed for our heart's desire and
got it, we then became convinced that this was a mere accident—that providential designs which had only some quite
different end just couldn't help throwing out this satisfaction
for us as a by-product—then the apparent bread would become a stone. A pretty stone, perhaps, or even a precious
stone. But not edible to the soul.

What we must fight against is Pope's maxim

> the first Almighty Cause
> Acts not by partial, but by general laws.

The odd thing is that Pope thought, and all who agree with
him think, that this philosophical theology is an advance beyond the religion of the child and the savage (and the New
Testament). It seems to them less *naïf* and anthropomorphic. The real difference, however, is that the an-
thropomorphism is more subtly hidden and of a far more
disastrous type.

For the implication is that there exists on the Divine level
a distinction with which we are very familiar on our own:
that between the plan (or the main plan) and its unintended
but unavoidable by-products. Whatever we do, even if it
achieves its object, will also scatter round it a spray of consequences which were not its object at all. This is so even in

private life. I throw out crumbs for the birds and provide, incidentally, a breakfast for the rats. Much more so in what may be called managerial life. The governing body of the college alters the time of dinner in hall; our object being to let the servants get home earlier. But by doing so we alter the daily pattern of life for every undergraduate. To some the new arrangement will be a convenience, to others the reverse. But we had no special favour for the first lot and no spite against the second. Our arrangement drags these unforeseen and undesired consequences after it. We can't help this.

On Pope's view God has to work in the same way. He has His grand design for the sum of things. Nothing we can say will deflect it. It leaves Him little freedom (or none?) for granting, or even for deliberately refusing, our prayers. The grand design churns out innumerable blessings and curses for individuals. God can't help that. They're all by-products.

I suggest that the distinction between plan and by-product must vanish entirely on the level of omniscience, omnipotence, and perfect goodness. I believe this because even on the human level it diminishes the higher you go. The better a human plan is made, the fewer unconsidered by-products it will have and the more birds it will kill with one stone, the more diverse needs and interests it will meet; the nearer it will come—it can never come very near—to being a plan for each individual. Bad laws make hard cases. But let us go beyond the managerial altogether. Surely a man of genius composing a poem or symphony must be less unlike God than a ruler? But the man of genius has no mere by-products in his work. Every note or word will be more than a means, more than a consequence. Nothing will be present *solely* for the sake of other things. If each note or word were conscious it would say, "The maker had me myself in view and chose for me, with the whole force of his genius, exactly the context I required." And it would be right—provided it remembered that every other note or word could say no less.

How should the true Creator work by "general laws"? "To generalise is to be an idiot," said Blake. Perhaps he went too far. But to generalise is to be a finite mind. Generalities are the lenses with which our intellects have to make do. How should God sully the infinite lucidity of this vision with such makeshifts? One might as well think He had to consult books of reference, or that, if He ever considered me individually, He would begin by saying, "Gabriel, bring me Mr. Lewis's file."

The God of the New Testament who takes into account the death of every sparrow is not more, but far less, anthropomorphic than Pope's.

I will not believe in the Managerial God and his general laws. If there is Providence at all, everything is providential and every providence is a special providence. It is an old and pious saying that Christ died not only for Man but for each man, just as much as if each had been the only man there was. Can I not believe the same of this creative act— which, as spread out in time, we call destiny or history? It is for the sake of each human soul. Each is an end. Perhaps for each beast. Perhaps even each particle of matter—the night sky suggests that the inanimate also has for God some value we cannot imagine. His ways are not (not there, anyway) like ours.

If you ask why I believe all this, I can only reply that we are taught, both by precept and example, to pray, and that prayer would be meaningless in the sort of universe Pope pictured. One of the purposes for which God instituted prayer may have been to bear witness that the course of events is not governed like a state but created like a work of art to which every being makes its contribution and (in prayer) a conscious contribution, and in which every being is both an end and a means. And since I have momentarily considered prayer itself as a means let me hasten to add that it is also an end. The world was made partly that there might be prayer; partly that our prayers for George might be answered. But let's have finished with "partly." The great work of art was made for the sake of all it does and is, down to the curve of every wave and the flight of every insect.

XI

I SEE you won't let me off. And the longer I look at it the less I shall like it. I must face—or else explicitly decline— the difficulties that really torment us when we cry for mercy in earnest. I have found no book that helps me with them all. I have so little confidence in my own power to tackle them that, if it were possible, I would let sleeping dogs lie. But the dogs are not sleeping. They are awake and snapping. We both bear the marks of their teeth. That being so, we had better share our bewilderments. By hiding them from each other we should not hide them from ourselves.

The New Testament contains embarrassing promises that what we pray for with faith we shall receive. Mark XI:24 is the most staggering. Whatever we ask for, believing that we'll get it, we'll get. No question, it seems, of confining it to spiritual gifts; *whatever* we ask for. No question of a merely general faith in God, but a belief that you will get the particular thing you ask. No question of getting either it or else something that is really far better for you; you'll get precisely it. And to heap paradox on paradox, the Greek doesn't even say "believing that you *will* get it." It uses the aorist, ἐλάβετε, which one is tempted to translate "believing that you *got* it." But this final difficulty I shall ignore. I don't expect Aramaic had anything which we—brought up on Latin grammar—would recognise as tenses at all.

How is this astonishing promise to be reconciled (a) With the observed facts? and (b) With the prayer in Gethsemane, and (as a result of that prayer) the universally accepted view that we should ask everything with a reservation ("if it be Thy will")?

As regards (a), no evasion is possible. Every war, every famine or plague, almost every death-bed, is the monument to a petition that was not granted. At this very moment thousands of people in this one island are facing as a *fait accompli* the very thing against which they have prayed night and day, pouring out their whole soul in prayer, and, as they thought, with faith. They have sought and not found. They have knocked and it has not been opened. "That which they greatly feared has come upon them."

But (b), though much less often mentioned, is surely an equal difficulty. How is it possible at one and the same moment to have a perfect faith—an untroubled or unhesitating faith as St. James says (I:6)—that you will get what you ask and yet also prepare yourself submissively in advance for a possible refusal? If you envisage a refusal as possible, how can you have simultaneously a perfect confidence that what you ask will not be refused? If you have that confidence, how can you take refusal into account at all?

It is easy to see why so much more is written about worship and contemplation than about "crudely" or "naïvely" petitionary prayer. They may be—I think they are—nobler forms of prayer. But they are also a good deal easier to write about.

As regards the first difficulty, I'm not asking why our petitions are so often refused. Anyone can see in general that this must be so. In our ignorance we ask what is not good for us or for others, or not even intrinsically possible. Or again, to grant one man's prayer involves refusing another's. There is much here which it is hard for our will to accept but nothing that is hard for our intellect to understand. The real problem is different; not why refusal is so frequent, but why the opposite result is so lavishly promised.

Shall we then proceed on Vidler's principles and scrap the embarrassing promises as "venerable archaisms" which have to be "outgrown"? Surely, even if there were no other objection, that method is too easy. If we are free to delete all inconvenient data we shall certainly have no theological difficulties; but for the same reason no solutions and no progress. The very writers of the detective stories, not to mention the scientists, know better. The troublesome fact, the apparent absurdity which can't be fitted in to any synthesis we have yet made, is precisely the one we must not ignore. Ten to one, it's in that cover the fox is lurking. There is always hope if we keep an unsolved problem fairly in view; there's none if we pretend it's not there.

Before going any further, I want to make two purely practical points.

1. These lavish promises are the worst possible place at which to begin Christian instruction in dealing with a child

or a Pagan. You remember what happened when the Widow started Huck Finn off with the idea he could get what he wanted by praying for it. He tried the experiment and then, not unnaturally, never gave Christianity a second thought; we had better not talk about the view of prayer embodied in Mark XI:24 as *"naïf"* or "elementary." If that passage contains a truth, it is a truth for very advanced pupils indeed. I don't think it is "addressed to our condition" (yours and mine) at all. It is a coping-stone, not a foundation. For most of us the prayer in Gethsemane is the only model. Removing mountains can wait.

2. We must not encourage in ourselves or others any tendency to work up a subjective state which, if we succeeded, we should describe as "faith," with the idea that this will somehow insure the granting of our prayer. We have probably all done this as children. But the state of mind which desperate desire working on a strong imagination can manufacture is not faith in the Christian sense. it is a feat of psychological gymnastics.

It seems to me we must conclude that such promises about prayer with faith refer to a degree or kind of faith which most believers never experience. A far inferior degree is, I hope, acceptable to God. Even the kind that says "Help thou my unbelief" may make way for a miracle. Again, the absence of such faith as insures the granting of the prayer is not even necessarily a sin; for Our Lord had no such assurance when He prayed in Gethsemane.

How or why does such faith occur sometimes, but not always, even in the perfect petitioner? We, or I, can only guess. My own idea is that it occurs only when the one who prays does so as God's fellow-worker, demanding what is needed for the joint work. It is the prophet's, the apostle's, the missionary's, the healer's prayer that is made with this confidence and finds the confidence justified by the event. The difference, we are told, between a servant and a friend is that a servant is not in his master's secrets. For him, "orders are orders." He has only his own surmises as to the plans he helps to execute. But the fellow-worker, the companion or (dare we say?) the colleague of God is so united with Him at certain moments that something of the divine foreknowledge enters his mind. Hence his faith is the "evidence"—that is, the evidentness, the obviousness—of things not seen.

As the friend is above the servant, the servant is above the suitor, the man praying on his own behalf. It is no sin to be a suitor. Our Lord descends into the humiliation of being a suitor, of praying on His own behalf, in Gethsemane. But when He does so the certitude about His Father's will is apparently withdrawn.

After that it would be no true faith—it would be idle presumption—for us, who are habitually suitors and do not often rise to the level of servants, to imagine that we shall have any assurance which is not an illusion—or correct only by accident—about the event of our prayers. Our struggle is —isn't it?—to achieve and retain faith on a lower level. To believe that, whether He can grant them or not, God will listen to our prayers, will take them into account. Even to go on believing that there is a Listener at all. For as the situation grows more and more desperate, the grisly fears intrude. Are we only talking to ourselves in an empty universe? The silence is often so emphatic. And we have prayed so much already.

What do you think about these things? I have offered only guesses.

XII

Mʏ experience is the same as yours. I have never met a book on prayer which was much use to people in our position. There are many little books *of* prayers, which may be helpful to those who share Rose Macaulay's approach, but you and I wouldn't know what to do with them. It's not words we lack! And there are books *on* prayer, but they nearly all have a strongly conventual background. Even the *Imitation* is sometimes, to an almost comic degree, "not addressed to my condition." The author assumes that you will want to be chatting in the kitchen when you ought to be in your cell. Our temptation is to be in our studies when we ought to be chatting in the kitchen. (Perhaps if our studies were as cold as those cells it would be different.)

You and I are people of the foothills. In the happy days when I was still a walker, I loved the hills, and even mountain walks, but I was no climber. I hadn't the head. So now, I do not attempt the precipices of mysticism. On the other hand, there is, apparently, a level of prayer-life lower even than ours. I don't mean that the people who occupy it are spiritually lower than we. They may far excel us. But their praying is of an astonishingly undeveloped type.

I have only just learned about it—from our Vicar. He assures me that, so far as he has been able to discover, the overwhelming majority of his parishioners mean by "saying their prayers" repeating whatever little formula they were taught in childhood by their mothers. I wonder how this can come about. It can't be that they are never penitent or thankful—they're dear people, many of them—or have no needs. Is it that there is a sort of water-tight bulk-head between their "religion" and their "real life," in which case the part of their life which they call "religious" is really the irreligious part?

But however badly needed a good book on prayer is, I shall never try to write it. Two people on the foothills comparing notes in private are all very well. But in a book one would inevitably seem to be attempting, not discussion, but instruction. And for me to offer the world instruction about prayer would be impudence.

About the higher level—the crags up which the mystics vanish out of my sight—the glaciers and the aiguilles—I have only two things to say. One is that I don't think we are all "called" to that ascent. "If it were so, He would have told us."

The second is this. The following position is gaining ground and is extremely plausible. Mystics (it is said) starting from the most diverse religious premises all find the

63

same things. These things have singularly little to do with the professed doctrines of any particular religion—Christianity, Hinduism, Buddhism, Neo-Platonism, etc. Therefore, mysticism is, by empirical evidence, the only real contact man has ever had with the unseen. The agreement of the explorers proves that they are all in touch with something objective. It is therefore the one true religion. And what we call the "religions" are either mere delusions or, at best, so many porches through which an entrance into transcendent reality can be effected.

> And when he hath the kernel eate,
> Who doth not throw away the shell?

I am doubtful about the premises. Did Plotinus and Lady Julian and St. John of the Cross really find "the same things?" Even admitting some similarity. One thing common to all mysticisms is the temporary shattering of our ordinary spatial and temporal consciousness and of our discursive intellect. The value of this negative experience must depend on the nature of that positive, whatever it is, for which it makes room. But should we not expect that the negative would always *feel* the same? If wine-glasses were conscious, I suppose that *being emptied* would be the same experience for each, even if some were to remain empty and some to be filled with poison and some broken. All who leave the land and put to sea will "find the same things"—the land sinking below the horizon, the gulls dropping behind, the salty breeze. Tourists, merchants, sailors, pirates, missionaries—it's all one. But this identical experience vouches for nothing about the utility or lawfulness or final event of their voyages.

> It may be that the gulfs will wash them down,
> It may be they will touch the Happy Isles.

I do not at all regard mystical experience as an illusion. I think it shows that there is a way to go, before death, out of what may be called "this world"—out of the stage set. Out of this; but into what? That's like asking an Englishman "Where does the sea lead to?" He will reply, "To everywhere on earth, including Davy Jones's locker, except England." The lawfulness, safety, and utility of the mystical voyage depends not at all on its being mystical—that is, on its being a departure—but on the motives, skill, and constancy of the voyager, and on the grace of God. The true religion gives value to its own mysticism; mysticism does not validate the religion in which it happens to occur.

I shouldn't be at all disturbed if it could be shown that a diabolical mysticism, or drugs, produced experiences indistinguishable (by introspection) from those of the great Christian mystics. Departures are all alike; it is the landfall that crowns the voyage. The saint, by being a saint, proves that his mysticism (if he was a mystic; not all saints are) led him aright; the fact that he has practised mysticism could never prove his sanctity.

You may wonder that my intense desire to peep behind the scenes has not led me to attempt the mystic way. But would it not be the worst of all possible motives? The saint may win a "mortal glimpse of death's immortal rose," but it is a by-product. He took ship simply in humble and selfless love.

There can be a desire (like mine) with no carnal element in it at all which is nevertheless, in St. Paul's sense, "flesh" and not "spirit." That is, there can be a merely impulsive, headstrong, greedy desire even for spiritual things. It is, like our other appetites, "cross-fodder." Yet, being crucified, it can be raised from the dead, and make part of our bliss.

Turning now to quite a different point in your letter. I

too had noticed that our prayers for others flow more easily than those we offer on our own behalf. And it would be nice to accept your view that this just shows we are made to live by charity. I'm afraid, however, I detect two much less attractive reasons for the ease of my own intercessory prayers. One is that I am often, I believe, praying for others when I should be doing things for them. It's so much easier to pray for a bore than to go and see him. And the other is like unto it. Suppose I pray that you may be given grace to withstand your besetting sin (short list of candidates for this post will be forwarded on demand). Well, all the work has to be done by God and you. If I pray against my own besetting sin there will be work for me. One sometimes fights shy of admitting an act to be a sin for this very reason.

The increasing list of people to be prayed for is, nevertheless, one of the burdens of old age. I have a scruple about crossing anyone off the list. When I say a scruple, I mean precisely a scruple. I don't really think that if one prays for a man at all it is a duty to pray for him all my life. But when it comes to dropping him *now,* this particular day, it somehow goes against the grain. And as the list lengthens, it is hard to make it more than a mere string of names. But here —in some measure—a curious law comes into play. Don't you find that, if you keep your mind fixed upon God, you will automatically think of the person you are praying for; but that there is no tendency for it to work the other way round?

XIII

I've just found in an old note-book a poem, with no author's name attached, which is rather relevant to something we were talking about a few weeks ago—I mean, the haunting fear that there is no-one listening, and that what we call prayer is soliloquy: someone talking to himself. This writer takes the bull by the horns and says in effect: "Very well, suppose it is," and gets a surprising result. Here is the poem.

> They tell me, Lord, that when I seem
> To be in speech with you,
> Since but one voice is heard, it's all a dream,
> One talker aping two.
>
> Sometimes it is, yet not as they
> Conceive it. Rather, I

Seek in myself the things I hoped to say,
    But lo!, my wells are dry.

Then, seeing me empty, you forsake
    The listener's role and through
My dumb lips breathe and into utterance wake
    The thoughts I never knew.

And thus you neither need reply
    Nor can; thus, while we seem
Two talkers, thou art One forever, and I
    No dreamer, but thy dream.

Dream makes it too like Pantheism and was perhaps dragged in for the rhyme. But is he not right in thinking that prayer in its most perfect state is a soliloquy? If the Holy Spirit speaks in the man, then in prayer God speaks to God. But the human petitioner does not therefore become a "dream." As you said the other day, God and man cannot exclude one another, as man excludes man, at the point of junction, so to call it, between Creator and creature; the point where the mystery of creation—timeless for God, and incessant in time for us—is actually taking place. "God did (or said) it" and "I did (or said) it" can both be true.

You remember the two maxims Owen [Barfield] lays down in *Saving the Appearances*? On the one hand, the man who does not regard God as other than himself cannot be said to have a religion at all. On the other hand, if I think God other than myself in the same way in which my fellowmen, and objects in general, are other than myself, I am beginning to make Him an idol. I am daring to treat His existence as somehow *parallel* to my own. But He is the ground of our being. He is always both within us and over against us.

Our reality is so much from His reality as He, moment by moment, projects into us. The deeper the level within ourselves from which our prayer, or any other act, wells up, the more it is His, but not at all the less ours. Rather, most ours when most His. Arnold speaks of us as "enisled" from one another in "the sea of life." But we can't be similarly "enisled" from God. To be discontinuous from God as I am discontinuous from you would be annihilation.

A question at once arises. Is it still God speaking when a liar or a blasphemer speaks? In one sense, almost Yes. Apart from God he could not speak at all; there are no words not derived from the Word; no acts not derived from Him who is *Actus purus*. And indeed the only way in which I can make real to myself what theology teaches about the heinousness of sin is to remember that every sin is the distortion of an energy breathed into us—an energy which, if not thus distorted, would have blossomed into one of those holy acts whereof "God did it" and "I did it" are both true descriptions. We poison the wine as He decants it into us; murder a melody He would play with us as the instrument. We caricature the self-portrait He would paint. Hence all sin, whatever else it is, is sacrilege.

We must, no doubt, distinguish this ontological continuity between Creator and creature which is, so to speak, "given" by the relation between them, from the union of wills which, under grace, is reached by a life of sanctity. The ontological continuity is, I take it, unchangeable, and exists between God and a reprobate (or a devil) no less than between God and a saint. "Whither shall I go then from thy presence? If I go down to hell, thou art there also."

Where there is prayer at all we may suppose that there is some effort, however feeble, towards the second condition, the union of wills. What God labours to do or say through the man comes back to God with a distortion which at any rate is not total.

Do you object to the apparent "roundaboutness"—it could easily be made comic—of the whole picture? Why should God speak to Himself through man? I ask, in reply, why should He do anything through His creatures? Why should He achieve, the long way round, through the labours of angels, men (always imperfectly obedient and efficient), and the activity of irrational and inanimate beings, ends which, presumably, the mere *fiat* of omnipotence would achieve with instantaneous perfection?

Creation seems to be delegation through and through. He will do nothing simply of Himself which can be done by creatures. I suppose this is because He is a giver. And He has nothing to give but Himself. And to give Himself is to do His deeds—in a sense, and on varying levels to be Himself —through the things He has made.

In Pantheism God is all. But the whole point of creation surely is that He was not content to be all. He intends to be "all *in all*."

One must be careful not to put this in a way which would blur the distinction between the creation of a man and the Incarnation of God. Could one, as a mere model, put it thus? In creation God makes—invents—a person and "utters"— injects—him into the realm of Nature. In the Incarnation, God the Son takes the body and human soul of Jesus, and, through that, the whole environment of Nature, all the creaturely predicament, into His own being. So that "He came down from Heaven" can almost be transposed into "Heaven drew earth up into it," and locality, limitation, sleep, sweat, footsore weariness, frustration, pain, doubt, and death, are, from before all worlds, known by God from within. The pure light walks the earth; the darkness, received into the heart of Deity, is there swallowed up. Where, except in uncreated light, can the darkness be drowned?

XIV

I won't admit without a struggle that when I speak of God "uttering" or "inventing" the creatures I am "watering down the concept of creation." I am trying to give it, by remote analogies, some sort of content. I know that to create is defined as "to make out of nothing," *ex nihilo*. But I take that to mean "*not* out of any pre-existing material." It can't mean that God makes what God has not thought of, or that He gives His creatures any powers or beauties which He Himself does not possess. Why, we think that even human work comes nearest to creation when the maker has "got it all out of his own head."

Nor am I suggesting a theory of "emanations." The differentia of an "emanation"—literally an overflowing, a trickling out—would be that it suggests something involuntary. But my words—"uttering" and "inventing"—are meant to suggest an act.

This act, as it is for God, must always remain totally inconceivable to man. For we—even our poets and musicians and inventors—never, in the ultimate sense, *make.* We only build. We always have materials to build from. All we can know about the act of creation must be derived from what we can gather about the relation of the creatures to their Creator.

Now the very Pagans knew that any beggar at your door might be a god in disguise: and the parable of the sheep and the goats is Our Lord's comment. What you do, or don't do, to the beggar, you do, or don't do, to Him. Taken at the Pantheist extreme, this could mean that men are only appearances of God—dramatic representations, as it were. Taken at the Legalist extreme, it could mean that God, by a sort of Legal fiction, will "deem" your kindness to the beggar a kindness done to Himself. Or again, as Our Lord's own words suggest, that since the least of men are His "brethren," the whole action is, so to speak, "within the family." And in what sense brethren? Biologically, because Jesus is Man? Ontologically, because the light lightens them all? Or simply "loved like brethren." (It cannot refer only to the regenerate.) I would ask first whether any one of these formulations is "right" in a sense which makes the others simply wrong? It seems to me improbable. If I ever see more clearly I will speak more surely.

Meanwhile, I stick to Owen's view. All creatures, from the angel to the atom, are other than God; with an otherness to which there is no parallel: incommensurable. The very words "to be" cannot be applied to Him and to them in exactly the same sense. But also, no creature is other than He in the same way in which it is other than all the rest. He is in it as they can never be in one another. In each of them as the ground and root and continual supply of its reality. And also in good rational creatures as light; in bad ones as fire, as at first the smouldering unease, and later the flaming anguish, of an unwelcome and vainly resisted presence.

Therefore of each creature we can say, "This also is Thou: neither is this Thou."

Simple faith leaps to this with astonishing ease. I once talked to a continental pastor who had seen Hitler, and had, by all human standards, good cause to hate him. "What did he look like?" I asked. "Like all men," he replied. "That is, like Christ."

One is always fighting on at least two fronts. When one is among Pantheists one must emphasise the distinctness, and relative independence, of the creatures. Among Deists—or perhaps in Woolwich, if the laity there really think God is to be sought in the sky—one must emphasise the divine presence in my neighbour, my dog, my cabbage-patch.

It is much wiser, I believe, to think of that presence in particular objects than just of "omnipresence." The latter gives very *naïf* people (Woolwich again, perhaps?) the idea of something spatially extended, like a gas. It also blurs the distinctions, the truth that God is present in each thing but not necessarily in the same mode; not in a man as in the consecrated bread and wine, nor in a bad man as in a good one, nor in a beast as in a man, nor in a tree as in a beast, nor in inanimate matter as in a tree. I take it there is a paradox here. The higher the creature, the more, and also the less, God is in it; the more present by grace, and the less present (by a sort of abdication) as mere power. By grace He gives the higher creatures power to will His will ("and wield their little tridents"): the lower ones simply execute it automatically.

It is well to have specifically holy places, and things, and days, for, without these focal points or reminders, the belief that all is holy and "big with God" will soon dwindle into a mere sentiment. But if these holy places, things, and days cease to remind us, if they obliterate our awareness that all ground is holy and every bush (could we but perceive it) a Burning Bush, then the hallows begin to do harm. Hence both the necessity, and the perennial danger, of "religion."

Boehme advises us once an hour "to fling ourselves beyond every creature." But in order to find God it is perhaps not always necessary to leave the creatures behind. We may ignore, but we can nowhere evade, the presence of God. The world is crowded with Him. He walks everywhere *incognito*. And the *incognito* is not always hard to penetrate. The real labour is to remember, to attend. In fact, to come awake. Still more, to remain awake.

Oddly enough, what corroborates me in this faith is the fact, otherwise so infinitely deplorable, that the awareness of this presence has so often been unwelcome. I call upon Him in prayer. Often He might reply—I think He does reply— "But you have been evading me for hours." For He comes not only to raise up but to cast down; to deny, to rebuke, to interrupt. The prayer "prevent us in all our doings" is often answered as if the word *prevent* had its modern meaning. The presence which we voluntarily evade is often, and we know it, His presence in wrath.

And out of this evil comes a good. If I never fled from His presence, then I should suspect those moments when I seemed to delight in it of being wish-fulfilment dreams. That, by the way, explains the feebleness of all those watered versions of Christianity which leave out all the darker elements and try to establish a religion of pure consolation. No real belief in the watered versions can last. Bemused and besotted as we are, we still dimly know at heart that nothing which is at all times and in every way agreeable to us can have objective reality. It is of the very nature of the real that it should have sharp corners and rough edges, that it should be resistant, should be itself. Dream-furniture is the only kind on which you never stub your toes or bang your knee. You and I have both known happy marriage. But how different our wives were from the imaginary mistresses of our adolescent dreams! So much less exquisitely adapted to all our wishes; and for that very reason (among others) so incomparably better.

Servile fear is, to be sure, the lowest form of religion. But a god such that there could never be occasion for even servile fear, a *safe* god, a tame god, soon proclaims himself to any sound mind as a fantasy. I have met no people who fully disbelieved in Hell and also had a living and life-giving belief in Heaven.

There is, I know, a belief in both, which is of no religious significance. It makes these spiritual things, or some travesty of them, objects of purely carnal, prudential, self-centred fear and hope. The deeper levels, those things which only immortal spirit can desire or dread, are not concerned at all. Such belief is fortunately very brittle. The old divines exhausted their eloquence especially in arousing such fear: but, as they themselves rather naïvely complain, the effect did not last for more than a few hours after the sermon.

The soul that has once been waked, or stung, or uplifted by the desire of God, will inevitably (I think) awake to the fear of losing Him.

I HADN'T realised that Betty was the silent third in this dia-
logue. I ought to have guessed it. Not that her worst enemy
ever accused her of being The Silent Woman—remember
the night at Mullingar—but that her silences during a prolonged argument between you and me are usually of a very
emphatic, audible, and even dialectical character. One knows
she is getting her broom ready and will soon sweep up all our
breakages. On the present point she is right. I *am* making
very heavy weather of what most believers find a very simple
matter. What is more natural, and easier, if you believe in
God, than to address Him? How could one not?

Yes. But it depends who one is. For those in my position—
adult converts from the *intelligentsia*—that simplicity and

spontaneity can't always be the starting point. One can't just jump back into one's childhood. If one tries to, the result will only be an archaising revival, like Victorian Gothic—a parody of being born again. We have to work back to the simplicity a long way round.

In actual practice, in my prayers, I often have to use that long way at the very beginning of the prayer.

St. François de Sales begins every meditation with the command *Mettez-vous en la présence de Dieu.* I wonder how many different mental operations have been carried out in intended obedience to that?

What happens to me if I try to take it—as Betty would tell me—"simply," is the juxtaposition of two "representations" or ideas or phantoms. One is the bright blur in the mind which stands for God. The other is the idea I call "me." But I can't leave it at that, because I know—and it's useless to pretend I don't know—that they are both phantasmal. The real I has created them both—or, rather, built them up in the vaguest way from all sorts of psychological odds and ends.

Very often, paradoxically, the first step is to banish the "bright blur"—or, in statelier language, to break the idol. Let's get back to what has at least some degree of resistant reality. Here are the four walls of the room. And here am I. But both terms are merely the façade of impenetrable mysteries.

The walls, they say, are matter. That is, as the physicists will try to tell me, something totally unimaginable, only mathematically describable, existing in a curved space, charged with appalling energies. If I could penetrate far enough into that mystery I should perhaps finally reach what is sheerly real.

And what am I? The façade is what I call consciousness.

I am at least conscious of the colour of those walls. I am not, in the same way, or to the same degree, conscious of what I call my thoughts: for if I try to examine what happens when I am thinking, it stops happening. Yet even if I could examine my thinking, it would, I well know, turn out to be the thinnest possible film on the surface of a vast deep. The psychologists have taught us that. Their real error lies in underestimating the depth and the variety of its contents. Dazzling lightness as well as dark clouds come up. And if all the enchanting visions are, as they rashly claim, mere disguises for sex, where lives the hidden artist who, from such monotonous and claustrophobic material, can make works of such various and liberating art? And depths of time too. All my past; my ancestral past; perhaps my pre-human past.

Here again, if I could dive deeply enough, I might again reach at the bottom that which simply is.

And only now am I ready, in my own fashion, to "place myself in the presence of God." Either mystery, if I could follow it far enough, would lead me to the same point—the point where something, in each case unimaginable, leaps forth from God's naked hand. The Indian, looking at the material world, says, "I am that." I say, "That and I grow from one root." *Verbum superne prodiens,* the Word coming forth from the Father, has made both, and brought them together in this subject-object embrace.

And what, you ask, is the advantage of all this? Well, for me—I am not talking about anyone else—it plants the prayer right in the present reality. For, whatever else is or is not real, this momentary confrontation of subject and object is certainly occurring: always occurring except when I am asleep. Here is the actual meeting of God's activity and man's —not some imaginary meeting that might occur if I were an angel or if God incarnate entered the room. There is here no question of a God "up there" or "out there"; rather, the present operation of God "in here," as the ground of my own being, and God "in there," as the ground of the matter that surrounds me, and God embracing and uniting both in the daily miracle of finite consciousness.

The two façades—the "I" as I perceive myself and the room as I perceive it—were obstacles as long as I mistook them for ultimate realities. But the moment I recognised them as façades, as mere surfaces, they became conductors. Do you see? A lie is a delusion only so long as we believe it; but a recognised lie is a reality—a real lie—and as such may be highly instructive. A dream ceases to be a delusion as soon as we wake. But it does not become a nonentity. It is a real dream: and it also may be instructive. A stage set is not a real wood or drawing room: it is a real stage set, and may be a good one. (In fact we should never ask of anything "Is it real?," for everything is real. The proper question is "A real *what?*," *e.g.,* a real snake or real *delirium tremens?*) The objects around me, and my idea of "me," will deceive if taken at their face value. But they are momentous if taken as the end-products of divine activities. Thus and not otherwise, the creation of matter and the creation of mind meet one another and the circuit is closed.

Or put it this way. I have called my material surroundings a stage set. A stage set is not a dream nor a nonentity. But if you attack a stage house with a chisel you will not get chips of brick or stone; you'll only get a hole in a piece of canvas and, beyond that, windy darkness. Similarly, if you start investigating the nature of matter, you will not find anything like what imagination has always supposed matter to be. You will get mathematics. From that unimaginable physical reality my senses select a few stimuli. These they translate or symbolise into sensations, which have no likeness at all to the reality of matter. Of these sensations my associative power, very much directed by my practical needs and influenced by social training, makes up little bundles into what I call "things" (labelled by nouns). Out of these I build myself a neat little box stage, suitably provided with properties such as hills, fields, houses, and the rest. In this I can act.

And you may well say "act." For what I call "myself" (for all practical, everyday purposes) is also a dramatic construction; memories, glimpses in the shaving glass, and snatches of the very fallible activity called "introspection" are the principal ingredients. Normally I call this construction "me," and the stage set "the real world."

Now the moment of prayer is for me—or involves for me as its condition—the awareness, the re-awakened awareness, that this "real world" and "real self" are very far from being rock-bottom realities. I cannot, in the flesh, leave the stage, either to go behind the scenes or to take my seat in the pit; but I can remember that these regions exist. And I also remember that my apparent self—this clown or hero or super —under his grease-paint is a real person with an off-stage life. The dramatic person could not tread the stage unless he concealed a real person: unless the real and unknown I existed, I would not even make mistakes about the imagined me. And in prayer this real I struggles to speak, for once, from his real being, and to address, for once, not the other actors, but—what shall I call Him? The Author, for He invented us all? The Producer, for He controls all? Or the Audience, for He watches, and will judge, the performance?

The attempt is not to escape from space and time and from my creaturely situation as a subject facing objects. It is more modest: to re-awake the awareness of that situation. If that can be done, there is no need to go anywhere else. This situation itself is, at every moment, a possible theophany. Here is the holy ground; the Bush is burning now.

Of course this attempt may be attended with almost every degree of success or failure. The prayer preceding all prayers is "May it be the real I who speaks. May it be the real Thou that I speak to." Infinitely various are the levels from which we pray. Emotional intensity is in itself no proof of spiritual depth. If we pray in terror we shall pray earnestly; it only proves that terror is an earnest emotion. Only God Himself can let the bucket down to the depths in us. And, on the other side, He must constantly work as the iconoclast. Every idea of Him we form, He must in mercy shatter. The most blessed result of prayer would be to rise thinking "But I never knew before. I never dreamed . . ." I suppose it was at such a moment that Thomas Aquinas said of all his own theology, "It reminds me of straw."

XVI

I DIDN'T mean that a "bright blur" is my only idea of God. I meant that something of that sort tends to be there when I start praying, and would remain if I made no effort to do better. And "bright blur" is not a very good description. In fact you can't have a good description of anything so vague. If the description became good it would become false.

Betty's recipe—"use images as the rest of us do"—doesn't help me much. And which does she mean? Images in the outer world, things made of wood or plaster? Or mental images?

As regards the first kind, I am not, as she suggests, suffering from a phobia about "idolatry." I don't think people of our type are in any danger of that. We shall always be aware that the image is only a bit of matter. But its use, for me, is very limited. I think the mere fact of keeping one's eyes focussed on something—almost any object will do—is some help towards concentration. The visual concentration symbolises, and promotes, the mental. That's one of the ways the body teaches the soul. The lines of a well-designed church, free from stunts, drawing one's eyes to the altar, have something of the same effect.

But I think that is all an image does for me. If I tried to get more out of it, I think it would get in the way. For one thing, it will have some artistic merits or (more probably) demerits. Both are a distraction. Again, since there can be no plausible images of the Father or the Spirit, it will usually be an image of Our Lord. The continual and exclusive addressing our prayers to Him surely tends to what has been called "Jesus-worship"? A religion which has its value; but not, in isolation, the religion Jesus taught.

Mental images may have the same defect, but they give rise to another problem as well.

St. Ignatius Loyola (I think it was) advised his pupils to begin their meditations with what he called a *compositio loci*. The Nativity or the Marriage at Cana, or whatever the theme might be, was to be visualised in the fullest possible detail. One of his English followers would even have us look up "what good Authors write of those places" so as to get the topography, "the height of the hills and the situation of the townes," correct. Now for two different reasons this is not "addressed to my condition."

One is that I live in an archaeological age. We can no longer, as St. Ignatius could, believingly introduce the clothes, furniture, and utensils of our own age into ancient Palestine. I'd know I wasn't getting them right. I'd know that the very sky and sunlight of those latitudes were different from any my northern imagination could supply. I could no doubt pretend to myself a naïveté I don't really possess; but that would cast an unreality over the whole exercise.

The second reason is more important. St. Ignatius was a great master, and I am sure he knew what his pupils needed. I conclude that they were people whose visual imagination was weak and needed to be stimulated. But the trouble with people like ourselves is the exact reverse. We can say this to one another because, in our mouths, it is not a boast but a confession. We are agreed that the power—indeed, the compulsion—to visualise is not "Imagination" in the higher sense, not the Imagination which makes a man either a great author or a sensitive reader. Ridden on a *very* tight rein, this visualising power can sometimes serve true Imagination; very often it merely gets in the way.

If I started with a *compositio loci* I should never reach the meditation. The picture would go on elaborating itself indefinitely and becoming every moment of less spiritual relevance.

There is indeed one mental image which does not lure me away into trivial elaborations. I mean the Crucifixion itself; not seen in terms of all the pictures and crucifixes, but as we must suppose it to have been in its raw, historical reality. But even this is of less spiritual value than one might expect. Compunction, compassion, gratitude—all the fruitful emotions—are strangled. Sheer physical horror leaves no room for them. Nightmare. Even so, the image ought to be periodically faced. But no one could live with it. It did not become a frequent motive of Christian art until the generations which had seen real crucifixions were all dead. As for many hymns and sermons on the subject—endlessly harping on blood, as if that were all that mattered—they must be the work either of people so far above me that they can't reach me, or else of people with no imagination at all. (Some might be cut off from me by both these gulfs.)

Yet mental images play an important part in my prayers. I doubt if any act of will or thought or emotion occurs in me without them. But they seem to help me most when they are most fugitive and fragmentary—rising and bursting like bubbles in champagne or wheeling like rooks in a windy sky: contradicting one another (in logic) as the crowded metaphors of a swift poet may do. Fix on any one, and it goes dead. You must do as Blake would do with a joy; kiss it as it flies. And then, in their total effect, they do mediate to me something very important. It is always something qualitative —more like an adjective than a noun. That, for me, gives it the impact of reality. For I think we respect nouns (and what we think they stand for) too much. All my deepest, and certainly all my earliest, experiences seem to be of sheer quality. The terrible and the lovely are older and solider than terrible and lovely things. If a musical phrase could be translated into words at all it would become an adjective. A great lyric is very like a long, utterly adequate, adjective. Plato was not so silly as the Moderns think when he elevated abstract nouns—that is, adjectives disguised as nouns—into the supreme realities—the Forms.

I know very well that in logic God is a "substance." Yet my thirst for quality is authorised even here: "We give thanks to thee for thy great glory." He *is* this glory. What He is (the quality) is no abstraction from Him. A personal God, to be sure; but so much more than personal. To speak more soberly, our whole distinction between "things" and "qualities," "substances" and "attitudes," has no application to Him. Perhaps it has much less than we suppose even to the created universe. Perhaps it is only part of the stage set.

The wave of images, thrown off like a spray from the

prayer, all momentary, all correcting, refining, "interinani-mating" one another, and giving a kind of spiritual body to the unimaginable, occurs more, I find, in acts of worship than in petitionary prayers. Of which, perhaps, we have written enough. But I don't regret it. They are the right starting point. They raise all the problems. If anyone attempted to practise, or to discuss, the higher forms without going through this turnstile, I should distrust him. "The higher does not stand without the lower." An omission or disdain of petition-ary prayer can sometimes, I think, spring not from superior sanctity but from a lack of faith and a consequent preference for levels where the question "Am I only doing things to my-self?" does not jut out in such apparent crudity.

XVII

IT's comical that you, of all people, should ask my views about prayer as worship or adoration. On this subject you yourself taught me nearly all I know. On a walk in the Forest of Dean. Can you have forgotten?

You first taught me the great principle "Begin where you are." I had thought one had to start by summoning up what we believe about the goodness and greatness of God, by thinking about creation and redemption and "all the blessings of this life." You turned to the brook and once more splashed your burning face and hands in the little waterfall and said, "Why not begin with this?"

And it worked. Apparently you have never guessed how much. That cushiony moss, that coldness and sound and dancing light were no doubt very minor blessings compared with "the means of grace and the hope of glory." But then they were manifest. So far as they were concerned, sight had replaced faith. They were not the hope of glory, they were an exposition of the glory itself.

Yet you were not—or so it seemed to me—telling me that "Nature," or "the beauties of Nature," manifest the glory. No such abstraction as "Nature" comes into it. I was learning the far more secret doctrine that *pleasures* are shafts of the glory as it strikes our sensibility. As it impinges on our will or our understanding, we give it different names—goodness or truth or the like. But its flash upon our senses and mood is pleasure.

But aren't there bad, unlawful pleasures? Certainly there are. But in calling them "bad pleasures" I take it we are using a kind of shorthand. We mean "pleasures snatched by unlawful acts." It is the stealing of the apple that is bad, not the sweetness. The sweetness is still a beam from the glory. That does not palliate the stealing. It makes it worse. There is sacrilege in the theft. We have abused a holy thing.

I have tried, since that moment, to make every pleasure into a channel of adoration. I don't mean simply by giving thanks for it. One must of course give thanks, but I mean something different. How shall I put it?

We can't—or I can't—hear the song of a bird simply as a sound. Its meaning or message ("That's a bird") comes with it inevitably—just as one can't see a familiar word in print as a merely visual pattern. The reading is as involuntary as the seeing. When the wind roars I don't just hear the roar; I "hear the wind." In the same way it is possible to "read" as well as to "have" a pleasure. Or not even "as well as." The distinction ought to become, and sometimes is, impossible; to receive it and to recognise its divine source are a single experience. This heavenly fruit is instantly redolent of the orchard where it grew. This sweet air whispers of the country from whence it blows. It is a message. We know we are being touched by a finger of that right hand at which there are pleasures for evermore. There need be no question of thanks or praise as a separate event, something done afterwards. To experience the tiny theophany is itself to adore.

Gratitude exclaims, very properly, "How good of God to give me this." Adoration says, "What must be the quality of that Being whose far-off and momentary coruscations are like this!" One's mind runs back up the sunbeam to the sun.

If I could always be what I aim at being, no pleasure would be too ordinary or too usual for such reception; from the first taste of the air when I look out of the window—one's whole cheek becomes a sort of palate—down to one's soft slippers at bed-time.

I don't always achieve it. One obstacle is inattention. Another is the wrong kind of attention. One could, if one practised, hear simply a roar and not the roaring-of-the-wind. In the same way, only far too easily, one can concentrate on the pleasure as an event in one's own nervous system—subjectify it—and ignore the smell of Deity that hangs about it. A third obstacle is greed. Instead of saying "This also is Thou," one may say the fatal word *Encore*. There is also conceit: the dangerous reflection that not everyone can find God in a plain slice of bread and butter, or that others would condemn as simply "grey" the sky in which I am delightedly observing such delicacies of pearl and dove and silver.

You notice that I am drawing no distinction between sensuous and aesthetic pleasures. But why should I? The line is almost impossible to draw and what use would it be if one succeeded in drawing it?

If this is Hedonism, it is also a somewhat arduous discipline. But it is worth some labour: for in so far as it succeeds, almost every day furnishes us with, so to speak, "bearings" on the Bright Blur. It becomes brighter but less blurry.

William Law remarks that people are merely "amusing themselves" by asking for the patience which a famine or a persecution would call for if, in the meantime, the weather and every other inconvenience sets them grumbling. One must learn to walk before one can run. So here. We—or at least I—shall not be able to adore God on the highest occasions if we have learned no habit of doing so on the lowest. At best, our faith and reason will tell us that He is adorable, but we shall not have *found* Him so, not have "tasted and seen." Any patch of sunlight in a wood will show you something about the sun which you could never get from reading books on astronomy. These pure and spontaneous pleasures are "patches of Godlight" in the woods of our experience.

Of course one wants the books too. One wants a great many things besides this "adoration in infinitesimals" which I am preaching. And if I were preaching it in public, instead of feeding it back to the very man who taught it me (though he may by now find the lesson nearly unrecognisable?), I should have to pack it in ice, enclose it in barbed-wire reservations, and stick up warning notices in every direction.

Don't imagine I am forgetting that the simplest act of mere obedience is worship of a far more important sort than what I've been describing (to obey is better than sacrifice). Or that God, besides being the Great Creator, is the Tragic Redeemer. Perhaps the Tragic Creator too. For I am not sure that the great canyon of anguish which lies across our lives is *solely* due to some pre-historic catastrophe. Something tragic may, as I think I've said before, be inherent in the very act of creation. So that one sometimes wonders why God thinks the game worth the candle. But then we share, in some degree, the cost of the candle and have not yet seen the "game."

There! I've done it again. I know that my tendency to use images like play and dance for the highest things is a stumbling-block to you. You don't, I admit, accuse it of profanity, as you used to—like the night we nearly came to blows at Edinburgh. You now, much more reasonably, call it "heartless." You feel it a brutal mockery of every martyr and every slave that a world-process which is so desperately serious to the actors should, at whatever celestial apex, be seen in terms of frivolities. And you add that it comes with a ludicrously ill grace from me, who never enjoyed any game and can dance no better than a centipede with wooden legs. But I still think you don't see the real point.

I do *not* think that the life of Heaven bears any analogy to play or dance in respect of frivolity. I do think that while we are in this "valley of tears," cursed with labour, hemmed round with necessities, tripped up with frustrations, doomed to perpetual plannings, puzzlings, and anxieties, certain qualities that must belong to the celestial condition have no chance to get through, can project no image of themselves, except in activities which, for us here and now, are frivolous. For surely we must suppose the life of the blessed to be an end in itself, indeed The End: to be utterly spontaneous; to be the complete reconciliation of boundless freedom with order—with the most delicately adjusted, supple, intricate, and beautiful order? How can you find any image of this in the "serious" activities either of our natural or of our (present) spiritual life? Either in our precarious and heartbroken affections or in the Way which is always, in some degree, a *via crucis?* No, Malcolm. It is only in our "hours-off," only in our moments of permitted festivity, that we find an analogy. Dance and game *are* frivolous, unimportant down here; for "down here" is not their natural place. Here, they are a moment's rest from the life we were placed here to live. But in this world everything is upside down. That which, if it could be prolonged here, would be a truancy, is likest that which in a better country is the End of ends. Joy is the serious business of Heaven.

XVIII

I PLEAD guilty. When I was writing about pleasures last week I had quite forgotten about the *mala mentis gaudia*— the pleasures of the mind which are intrinsically evil. The pleasure, say, of having a grievance. What a disappointment it is—for one self-revealing moment—to discover that the other party was not really to blame? And how a resentment, while it lasts, draws one back and back to nurse and fondle and encourage it! It behaves just like a lust. But I don't think this leaves my theory (and experience) of ordinary pleasures in ruins. Aren't these intrinsically vicious pleasures, as Plato said, "mixed"? To use his own image, given the itch, one wants to scratch it. And if you abstain, the temptation is very severe, and if you scratch there is a sort of pleasure in the momentary and deceptive relief. But one didn't want to itch. The scratch is not a pleasure simply, but only by comparison with the context. In the same way, resentment is pleasant only as a relief from, or alternative to, humiliation. I still think that those experiences which are pleasures in their own right can all be regarded as I suggest.

The mere mention of the horrible pleasures—the dainties of Hell—very naturally led you away from the subject of adoration to that of repentance. I'm going to follow you into your digression, for you said something I disagreed with.

I admit of course that penitential prayers—"acts" of penitence, as I believe they are called—can be on very different levels. At the lowest, what you call "Pagan penitence," there is simply the attempt to placate a supposedly angry power— "I'm sorry. I won't do it again. Let me off this time." At the highest level, you say, the attempt is, rather, to restore an infinitely valued and vulnerable personal relation which has been shattered by an action of one's own, and if forgiveness, in the "crude" sense of remission of penalty, comes in, this is valued chiefly as a symptom or seal or even by-product of the reconciliation. I expect you are right about that. I say "expect" because I can't claim to know much by experience about the highest level either of penitence or of anything else. The ceiling, if there is one, is a long way off.

All the same, there is a difference between us. I can't agree to call your lowest level "Pagan penitence." Doesn't your description cover a great deal of Old Testament penitence? Look at the Psalms. Doesn't it cover a good deal of Christian penitence—a good deal that is embodied in Christian liturgies? "Neither take thou vengeance for our sins . . . be not angry with us forever . . . *neque secundum iniquitates nostras retribuas nobis.*"

Here, as nearly always, what we regard as "crude" and "low," and what presumably is in fact lowest, spreads far further up the Christian life than we like to admit. And do we find anywhere in Scripture or in the Fathers that explicit and resounding rejection of it which would be so welcome?

I fully grant you that "wrath" can be attributed to God only by an analogy. The situation of the penitent before God isn't, but is somehow like, that of one appearing before a justly angered sovereign, lover, father, master, or teacher. But what more can we know about it than just this likeness? Trying to get in behind the analogy, you go further and fare worse. You suggest that what is traditionally regarded as our experience of God's anger would be more helpfully regarded as what inevitably happens to us if we behave inappropriately towards a reality of immense power. As you say, "The live wire doesn't feel angry with us, but if we blunder against it we get a shock."

My dear Malcolm, what do you suppose you have gained by substituting the image of a live wire for that of angered majesty? You have shut us all up in despair; for the angry can forgive, and electricity can't.

And you give as your reason that "even by analogy the sort of pardon which arises because a fit of temper is spent cannot worthily be attributed to God nor gratefully accepted by man." But the belittling words "fit of temper" are your own choice. Think of the fullest reconciliation between mortals. Is cool disapproval coolly assuaged? Is the culprit let down lightly in view of "extenuating circumstances"? Was peace restored by a moral lecture? Was the offence said not to "matter"? Was it hushed up or passed over? Blake knew better:

> I was angry with my friend:
> I told my wrath, my wrath did end.

> I was angry with my foe:
> I told it not, my wrath did grow.

You too know better. Anger—no peevish fit of temper, but just, generous, scalding indignation—passes (not necessarily at once) into embracing, exultant, re-welcoming love. That is how friends and lovers are truly reconciled. Hot wrath, hot love. Such anger is the fluid that love bleeds when you cut it. The *angers,* not the measured remonstrances, of lovers are love's renewal. Wrath and pardon are both, as applied to God, analogies; but they belong together to the same circle of analogy—the circle of life, and love, and deeply personal relationships. All the liberalising and "civilising" analogies only lead us astray. Turn God's wrath into mere enlightened disapproval, and you also turn His love into mere humanitarianism. The "consuming fire" and the "perfect beauty" both vanish. We have, instead, a judicious headmistress or a conscientious magistrate. It comes of being high-minded.

I know that "the wrath of man worketh not the righteousness of God." That is not because wrath is wrath but because man is (fallen) man.

But perhaps I've already said too much. All that any imagery can do is to facilitate, or at least not to impede, man's act of penitence and reception of pardon. We cannot see the matter "from God's side."

The crude picture of penitence as something like apology or even placation has, for me, the value of making penitence an act. The more high-minded views involve some danger of regarding it simply as a state of feeling. Do you agree that this would be unwholesome?

The question is before my mind at present because I've been reading Alexander Whyte. Morris lent him to me. He was a Presbyterian divine of the last century, whom I'd never heard of. Very well worth reading, and strangely broad-minded—Dante, Pascal, and even Newman, are among his heroes. But I mention him at the moment for a different reason. He brought me violently face to face with a characteristic of Puritanism which I had almost forgotten. For him, one essential symptom of the regenerate life is a permanent, and permanently horrified, perception of one's natural and (it seems) unalterable corruption. The true Christian's nostril is to be continually attentive to the inner cesspool. I knew that the experience was a regular feature of the old conversion stories. As in *Grace Abounding*: "But my inward and original corruption . . . that I had the guilt of to amazement . . . I was more loathsom in mine own eyes than was a toad . . . sin and corruption, I said, would as naturally bubble out of my heart, as water would bubble out of a fountain." Another author, quoted in Haller's *Rise of Puritanism,* says that when he looked into his heart, it was "as if I had in the heat of summer lookt down into the Filth of a Dungeon, where I discerned Millions of crawling living things in the midst of that Sink and liquid Corruption."

I won't listen to those who describe that vision as merely pathological. I have seen the "slimy things that crawled with legs" in my own dungeon. I thought the glimpse taught me sense. But Whyte seems to think it should be not a glimpse but a daily, lifelong scrutiny. Can he be right? It sounds so very unlike the New Testament fruits of the spirit—love, joy, peace. And very unlike the Pauline programme; "forgetting those things which are behind and reaching forth unto those things that are before." And very unlike St. François de Sales' green, dewy chapter on *la douceur* towards one's self. Anyway, what's the use of laying down a programme of permanent emotions? They can be permanent only by being factitious.

What do you think? I know that a spiritual emetic at the right moment may be needed. But not a regular diet of emetics! If one survived, one would develop a "tolerance" of them. This poring over the "sink" might breed its own perverse pride

> over-just and self-displeased
> For self-offence more than for God offended.

Anyway, in solitude, and also in confession, I have found (to my regret) that the degrees of shame and disgust which I actually feel at my own sins do not at all correspond to what my reason tells me about their comparative gravity. Just as the degree to which, in daily life, I feel the emotion of fear has very little to do with my rational judgement of the danger. I'd sooner have really nasty seas when I'm in an open boat than look down in perfect (actual) safety from the edge of a cliff. Similarly, I have confessed ghastly uncharities with less reluctance than small unmentionables—or those sins which happen to be ungentlemanly as well as un-Christian. Our emotional reactions to our own behaviour are of limited ethical significance.

TELL Betty that if you hadn't whisked me off onto the subject of repentance, I was just going to say the very thing she blames me for not saying. I was going to say that in adoration, more than in any other kind of prayer, the public or communal act is of the utmost importance. One would lose incomparably more by being prevented from going to church on Easter than on Good Friday. And, even in private, adoration should be communal—"with angels and archangels and all the company," all the transparent publicity of Heaven. On the other hand, I find that the prayers to which I can most fully attend in church are always those I have most often used in my bedroom.

I deny, with some warmth, the charge of being "choosy

about services." My whole point was that any form will do me if only I'm given time to get used to it. The idea of allowing myself to be put off by mere inadequacy—an ugly church, a gawky server, a badly turned-out celebrant—is horrible. On the contrary, it constantly surprises me how little these things matter, as if

> never anything can be amiss
> When simpleness and duty tender it.

One of the golden Communions of my life was in a Nisson hut. Sometimes the cockney accent of a choir has a singularly touching quality. A tin mug for a chalice, if there were good reason for it, would not distress me in the least. (I wonder what sort of crockery was used at the Last Supper?)

You ask me why I've never written anything about the Holy Communion. For the very simple reason that I am not good enough at Theology. I have nothing to offer. Hiding any light I think I've got under a bushel is not my besetting sin! I am much more prone to prattle unseasonably. But there is a point at which even I would gladly keep silent. The trouble is that people draw conclusions even from silence. Someone said in print the other day that I seemed to "admit rather than welcome" the sacraments.

I wouldn't like you and Betty to think the same. But as soon as I try to tell you anything more, I see another reason for silence. It is almost impossible to state the negative effect which certain doctrines have on me—my failure to be nourished by them—without seeming to mount an attack against them. But the very last thing I want to do is to unsettle in the mind of any Christian, whatever his denomination, the concepts—for him traditional—by which he finds it profitable to represent to himself what is happening when he receives the bread and wine. I could wish that no definitions had ever been felt to be necessary; and, still more, that none had been allowed to make divisions between churches.

Some people seem able to discuss different theories of this act as if they understood them all and needed only evidence as to which was best. This light has been withheld from me. I do not know and can't imagine what the disciples understood Our Lord to mean when, His body still unbroken and His blood unshed, He handed them the bread and wine, saying *they* were His body and blood. I can find within the forms of my human understanding no connection between eating a man—and it is as Man that the Lord has flesh—and entering into any spiritual oneness or community or κοινωνία with him. And I find "substance" (in Aristotle's sense), when stripped of its own accidents and endowed with the accidents of some other substance, an object I cannot think. My effort to do so produces mere nursery-thinking—a picture of something like very rarefied plasticine. On the other hand, I get on no better with those who tell me that the elements are mere bread and mere wine, used symbolically to remind me of the death of Christ. They are, on the natural level, such a very odd symbol of *that*. But it would be profane to suppose that they are as arbitrary as they seem to me. I well believe there is in reality an appropriateness, even a necessity, in their selection. But it remains, for me, hidden. Again, if they are, if the whole act is, simply memorial, it would seem to follow that its value must be purely psychological, and dependent on the recipient's sensibility at the moment of reception. And I cannot see why *this* particular reminder—a hundred other things may, psychologically, remind me of Christ's death, equally, or perhaps more—should be so uniquely important as all Christendom (and my own heart) unhesitatingly declare.

However, then, it may be for others, for me the something

which holds together and "informs" all the objects, words, and actions of this rite is unknown and unimaginable. I am not saying to anyone in the world, "Your explanation is wrong." I am saying, "Your explanation leaves the mystery for me still a mystery."

Yet I find no difficulty in believing that the veil between the worlds, nowhere else (for me) so opaque to the intellect, is nowhere else so thin and permeable to divine operation. Here a hand from the hidden country touches not only my soul but my body. Here the prig, the don, the modern in me have no privilege over the savage or the child. Here is big medicine and strong magic. *Favete linguis.*

When I say "magic" I am not thinking of the paltry and pathetic techniques by which fools attempt and quacks pretend to control nature. I mean rather what is suggested by fairy-tale sentences like "This is a magic flower, and if you carry it the seven gates will open to you of their own accord," or "This is a magic cave and those who enter it will renew their youth." I should define magic in this sense as "objective efficacy which cannot be further analysed."

Magic, in this sense, will always win a response from a normal imagination because it is in principle so "true to nature." Mix these two powders and there will be an explosion. Eat a grain of this and you will die. Admittedly, the "magical" element in such truths can be got rid of by explanation; that is, by seeing them to be instances or consequences of larger truths. Which larger truths remain "magical" till they also are, in the same way, explained. In that fashion, the sciences are always pushing further back the realm of mere "brute fact." But no scientist, I suppose, believes that the process could ever reach completion. At the very least, there must always remain the utterly "brute" fact, the completely opaque *datum,* that a universe—or, rather, *this* universe with its determinate character—exists; as "magical" as the magic flower in the fairy-tale.

Now the value, for me, of the magical element in Christianity is this. It is a permanent witness that the heavenly realm, certainly no less than the natural universe and perhaps very much more, is a realm of objective facts—hard, determinate facts, not to be constructed *a priori,* and not to be dissolved into maxims, ideals, values, and the like. One cannot conceive a more completely "given," or, if you like, a more "magical," fact than the existence of God as *causa sui.*

Enlightened people want to get rid of this magical element in favour of what they would call the "spiritual" element. But the spiritual, conceived as something thus antithetical to "magical," seems to become merely the psychological or ethical. And neither that by itself, nor the magical by itself, is a religion. I am not going to lay down rules as to the share—quantitatively considered—which the magical should have in anyone's religious life. Individual differences may be permissible. What I insist on is that it can never be reduced to zero. If it is, what remains is only morality, or culture, or philosophy.

What makes some theological works like sawdust to me is the way the authors can go on discussing how far certain positions are adjustable to contemporary thought, or beneficial in relation to social problems, or "have a future" before them, but never squarely ask what grounds we have for supposing them to be true accounts of any objective reality. As if we were trying to make rather than to learn. Have we no Other to reckon with?

I hope I do not offend God by making my Communions in the frame of mind I have been describing. The command, after all, was Take, eat: not Take, understand. Particularly, I hope I need not be tormented by the question "What is this?"—this wafer, this sip of wine. That has a dreadful effect on me. It invites me to take "this" out of its holy context and regard it as an object among objects, indeed as part of nature. It is like taking a red coal out of the fire to examine it: it becomes a dead coal. To me, I mean. All this is autobiography, not theology.

XX

I REALLY must digress to tell you a bit of good news. Last week, while at prayer, I suddenly discovered—or felt as if I did—that I had really forgiven someone I have been trying to forgive for over thirty years. Trying, and praying that I might. When the thing actually happened—sudden as the longed-for cessation of one's neighbour's radio—my feeling was "But it's so easy. Why didn't you do it ages ago?" So many things are done easily the moment you can do them at all. But till then, sheerly impossible, like learning to swim. There are months during which no efforts will keep you up; then comes the day and hour and minute after which, and ever after, it becomes almost impossible to sink. It also seemed to me that forgiving (that man's cruelty) and being forgiven (my resentment) were the very same thing. "Forgive and you shall be forgiven" sounds like a bargain. But perhaps it is something much more. By heavenly standards, that is, for pure intelligence, it is perhaps a tautology—forgiving and being forgiven are two names for the same thing. The important thing is that a discord has been resolved, and it is certainly the great Resolver who has done it. Finally, and perhaps best of all, I believed anew what is taught us in the parable of the Unjust Judge. No evil habit is so ingrained nor so long prayed against (as it seemed) in vain, that it cannot, even in dry old age, be whisked away.

I wonder do the long dead know it when we at last, after countless failures, succeed in forgiving them? It would be a pity if they don't. A pardon given but not received would be frustrated. Which brings me to your question.

Of course I pray for the dead. The action is so spontaneous, so all but inevitable, that only the most compulsive theological case against it would deter me. And I hardly know how the rest of my prayers would survive if those for the dead were forbidden. At our age the majority of those we love best are dead. What sort of intercourse with God could I have if what I love best were unmentionable to Him?

On the traditional Protestant view, all the dead are damned or saved. If they are damned, prayer for them is useless. If they are saved, it is equally useless. God has already done all for them. What more should we ask?

But don't we believe that God has already done and is already doing all that He can for the living? What more should we ask? Yet we are told to ask.

"Yes," it will be answered, "but the living are still on the road. Further trials, developments, possibilities of error, await them. But the saved have been made perfect. They have finished the course. To pray for them presupposes that progress and difficulty are still possible. In fact, you are bringing in something like Purgatory."

Well, I suppose I am. Though even in Heaven some perpetual increase of beatitude, reached by a continually more ecstatic self-surrender, without the possibility of failure but not perhaps without its own ardours and exertions—for delight also has its severities and steep ascents, as lovers know —might be supposed. But I won't press, or guess, that side for the moment. I believe in Purgatory.

Mind you, the Reformers had good reasons for throwing doubt on "the Romish doctrine concerning Purgatory" as that Romish doctrine had then become. I don't mean merely the commercial scandal. If you turn from Dante's *Purgatorio* to the sixteenth century you will be appalled by the degradation. In Thomas More's *Supplication of Souls* Purgatory is simply temporary Hell. In it the souls are tormented by devils, whose presence is "more horrible and grievous to us than is the pain itself." Worse still, Fisher, in his Sermon on Psalm VI, says the tortures are so intense that the spirit who suffers them cannot, for pain, "remember God as he ought to do." In fact, the very etymology of the word *purgatory* has dropped out of sight. Its pains do not bring us nearer to God, but make us forget Him. It is a place not of purification but purely of retributive punishment.

The right view returns magnificently in Newman's *Dream*. There, if I remember it rightly, the saved soul, at the very foot of the throne, begs to be taken away and cleansed. It cannot bear for a moment longer "With its darkness to affront that light." Religion has reclaimed Purgatory.

Our souls *demand* Purgatory, don't they? Would it not break the heart if God said to us, "It is true, my son, that your breath smells and your rags drip with mud and slime, but we are charitable here and no one will upbraid you with these things, nor draw away from you. Enter into the joy"? Should we not reply, "With submission, sir, and if there is no objection, I'd *rather* be cleaned first." "It may hurt, you know"—"Even so, sir."

I assume that the process of purification will normally involve suffering. Partly from tradition; partly because most real good that has been done me in this life has involved it. But I don't think suffering is the purpose of the purgation. I can well believe that people neither much worse nor much better than I will suffer less than I or more. "No nonsense about merit." The treatment given will be the one required, whether it hurts little or much.

My favourite image on this matter comes from the dentist's chair. I hope that when the tooth of life is drawn and I am "coming round," a voice will say, "Rinse your mouth out with this." *This* will be Purgatory. The rinsing may take longer than I can now imagine. The taste of *this* may be more fiery and astringent than my present sensibility could endure. But More and Fisher shall not persuade me that it will be disgusting and unhallowed.

Your own peculiar difficulty—that the dead are not in time—is another matter.

How do you know they are not? I certainly believe that to be God is to enjoy an infinite present, where nothing has yet passed away and nothing is still to come. Does it follow that we can say the same of saints and angels? Or at any rate exactly the same? The dead might experience a time which was not quite so linear as ours—it might, so to speak, have thickness as well as length. Already in this life we get some thickness whenever we learn to attend to more than one thing at once. One can suppose this increased to any extent, so that though, for them as for us, the present is always be-coming the past, yet each present contains unimaginably more than ours.

I *feel*—can you work it out for me and tell me if it is more than a feeling?—that to make the life of the blessed dead strictly timeless is inconsistent with the resurrection of the body.

Again, as you and I have agreed, whether we pray on be-half of the living or the dead, the causes which will prevent or exclude the events we pray for are in fact already at work. Indeed they are part of a series which, I suppose, goes back as far as the creation of the universe. The causes which made George's illness a trivial one were already operating while we prayed about it; if it had been what we feared, the causes of that would have been operative. That is why, as I hold, our prayers are granted, or not, in eternity. The task of dovetailing the spiritual and physical histories of the world into each other is accomplished in the total act of creation it-self. Our prayers, and other free acts, are known to us only as we come to the moment of doing them. But they are eter-nally in the score of the great symphony. Not "pre-deter-mined"; the syllable *pre* lets in the notion of eternity as sim-ply an older time. For though we cannot experience our life as an endless present, we are eternal in God's eyes; that is, in our deepest reality. When I say we are "in time" I don't mean that we are, impossibly, outside the endless present in which He beholds us as He beholds all else. I mean, our creaturely limitation is that our fundamentally timeless reality can be experienced by us only in the mode of suc-cession.

In fact we began by putting the question wrongly. The question is not whether the dead are part of timeless reality.

They are; so is a flash of lightning. The question is whether they share the divine perception of timelessness.

Tell George I should be delighted. *Rendezvous* in my rooms at 7:15. We do *not* dress for dinner on ordinary nights.

XXI

Betty is quite right—"all this about prayer and never a word on the practical problem: its irksomeness." And she sees fit to add, "Anyone might think it was a correspondence between two saints!"

That was a barbed shaft and went home. And yet I don't really think we were being hypocritical. Doesn't the mere fact of putting something into words of itself involve an exaggeration? Prose words, I mean. Only poetry can speak low enough to catch the faint murmur of the mind, the "litel winde, unethe hit might be lesse." The other day I tried to describe to you a very minimal experience—the tiny wisps of adoration with which (sometimes) I salute my pleasures. But I now see that putting it down in black and white made it sound far bigger than it really is. The truth is, I haven't any language weak enough to depict the weakness of my spiritual life. If I weakened it enough it would cease to be language at all. As when you try to turn the gas-ring a little lower still, and it merely goes out.

Then again, by talking at this length about prayer at all, we seem to give it a much bigger place in our lives than, I'm afraid, it has. For while we talk about it, all the rest of our experience, which in reality crowds our prayer into the margin or sometimes off the page altogether, is not mentioned. Hence, in the talk, an error of proportion which amounts to, though it was not intended for, a lie.

Well, let's now at any rate come clean. Prayer is irksome. An excuse to omit it is never unwelcome. When it is over, this casts a feeling of relief and holiday over the rest of the day. We are reluctant to begin. We are delighted to finish. While we are at prayer, but not while we are reading a novel or solving a cross-word puzzle, any trifle is enough to distract us.

And we know that we are not alone in this. The fact that prayers are constantly set as penances tells its own tale.

The odd thing is that this reluctance to pray is not confined to periods of dryness. When yesterday's prayers were full of comfort and exaltation, today's will still be felt as, in some degree, a burden.

Now the disquieting thing is not simply that we skimp and begrudge the duty of prayer. The really disquieting thing is it should have to be numbered among duties at all. For we believe that we were created "to glorify God and enjoy Him forever." And if the few, the very few, minutes we now spend on intercourse with God are a burden to us rather than a delight, what then? If I were a Calvinist this symptom would fill me with despair. What can be done *for*—or what should

113

be done *with*—a rose-tree that *dislikes* producing roses? Surely it ought to want to?

Much of our backwardness in prayer is no doubt due to our sins, as every teacher will tell us; to our avoidable immersion in the things of this world, to our neglect of mental discipline. And also to the very worst kind of "fear of God." We shrink from too naked a contact, because we are afraid of the divine demands upon us which it might make too audible. As some old writer says, many a Christian prays faintly "lest God might really hear him, which he, poor man, never intended." But sins—at any rate, our actual and individual sins—are not perhaps the only cause.

By the very constitution of our minds as they now are—whatever they may have been when God first made man—it is difficult for us to concentrate on anything which is neither sensible (like potatoes) nor abstract (like numbers). What is concrete but immaterial can be kept in view only by painful effort. Some would say "Because it does not exist." But the rest of our experience cannot accept that solution. For we ourselves and all that we most care about seem to come in the class "concrete (that is, individual) and insensible." If reality consists of nothing but physical objects and abstract concepts, then reality has, in the last resort, nothing to say to us. We are in the wrong universe. Man is a *passion inutile;* and so, good night. And yet, the supposedly real universe has been quarried out of man's sensuous experiences.

The painful effort which prayer involves is no proof that we are doing something we were not created to do.

If we were perfected, prayer would not be a duty, it would be delight. Some day, please God, it will be. The same is true of many other behaviours which now appear as duties. If I loved my neighbour as myself, most of the actions which are now my moral duty would flow out of me as spontaneously as song from a lark or fragrance from a flower. Why is this not so yet? Well, we know, don't we? Aristotle has taught us that delight is the "bloom" on an unimpeded activity. But the very activities for which we were created are, while we live on earth, variously impeded: by evil in ourselves or in others. Not to practise them is to abandon our humanity. To practise them spontaneously and delightfully is not yet possible. This situation creates the category of duty, the whole specifically *moral* realm.

It exists to be transcended. Here is the paradox of Christianity. As practical imperatives for here and now the two great commandments have to be translated "Behave as *if you* loved God and man." For no man can love because he is told to. Yet obedience on this practical level is not really obedience at all. And if a man really loved God and man, once again this would hardly be obedience; for if he did, he would be unable to help it. Thus the command really says to us, "Ye must be born again." Till then, we have duty, morality, the Law. A schoolmaster, as St. Paul says, to bring us to Christ. We must expect no more of it than of a schoolmaster; we must allow it no less. I must say my prayers to-day whether I feel devout or not; but that is only as I must learn my grammar if I am ever to read the poets.

But the school-days, please God, are numbered. There is no morality in Heaven. The angels never knew (from within) the meaning of the word *ought,* and the blessed dead have long since gladly forgotten it. This is why Dante's Heaven is so right, and Milton's, with its military discipline, so silly. This also explains—to pick up an earlier point— why we have to picture that world in terms which seem almost frivolous. In this world our most momentous actions are impeded. We can picture unimpeded, and therefore delighted, action only by the analogy of our present play and leisure. Thus we get the notion that what is as free as they would have to matter as little.

I said, mind you, that "most" of the behaviour which is now duty would be spontaneous and delightful if we were, so to speak, good rose-trees. Most, not all. There is, or might be, martyrdom. We are not called upon to like it. Our Master didn't. But the principle holds, that duty is always conditioned by evil. Martyrdom, by the evil in the persecutor; other duties, by lack of love in myself or by the general diffused evil of the world. In the perfect and eternal world the Law will vanish. But the results of having lived faithfully under it will not.

I am therefore not really deeply worried by the fact that prayer is at present a duty, and even an irksome one. This is humiliating. It is frustrating. It is terribly time-wasting—the worse one is praying, the longer one's prayers take. But we are still only at school. Or, like Donne, "I tune my instrument here at the door." And even now—how can I weaken the words enough, how speak at all without exaggeration?—we have what seem rich moments. Most frequently, perhaps, in our momentary, only just voluntary, ejaculatʻons; refreshments "unimplored, unsought, Happy for man so coming."

But I don't rest much on that; nor would I if it were ten times as much as it is. I have a notion that what seem our worst prayers may really be, in God's eyes, our best. Those, I mean, which are least supported by devotional feeling and contend with the greatest disinclination. For these, perhaps, being nearly all will, come from a deeper level than feeling. In feeling there is so much that is really not ours—so much that comes from weather and health or from the last book read. One thing seems certain. It is no good angling for the rich moments. God sometimes seems to speak to us most intimately when He catches us, as it were, off our guard. Our preparations to receive Him sometimes have the opposite effect. Doesn't Charles Williams say somewhere that "the altar must often be built in one place in order that the fire from heaven may descend *somewhere else*"?

XXII

B Y not belonging to a press-cutting agency I miss most of the bouquets and brickbats which are aimed at me. So I never saw the article you write about. But I have seen others of that kind, and they'll break no bones of mine. Don't, however, misjudge these "liberal Christians." They genuinely believe that writers of my sort are doing a great deal of harm.

They themselves find it impossible to accept most of the articles of the "faith once given to the saints." They are nevertheless extremely anxious that some vestigial religion which they (not we) can describe as "Christianity" should continue to exist and make numerous converts. They think these converts will come in only if this religion is sufficiently "demythologised." The ship must be lightened if she is to keep afloat.

It follows that, to them, the most mischievous people in the world are those who, like myself, proclaim that Christianity essentially involves the supernatural. They are quite sure that belief in the supernatural never will, nor should, be revived, and that if we convince the world that it must choose between accepting the supernatural and abandoning all pretence of Christianity, the world will undoubtedly choose the second alternative. It will thus be we, not the liberals, who have really sold the pass. We shall have re-attached to the name *Christian* a deadly scandal from which, but for us, they might have succeeded in decontaminating it.

If, then, some tone of resentment creeps into their comments on our work, can you blame them? But it would be unpardonable if we allowed ourselves any resentment against them. We do in some measure queer their pitch. But they make no similar contribution to the forces of secularism. It has already a hundred champions who carry far more weight than they. Liberal Christianity can only supply an ineffectual echo to the massive chorus of agreed and admitted unbelief. Don't be deceived by the fact that this echo so often "hits the headlines." That is because attacks on Christian doctrine which would pass unnoticed if they were launched (as they are daily launched) by anyone else, become News when the attacker is a clergyman; just as a very commonplace protest against make-up would be News if it came from a film star.

By the way, did you ever meet, or hear of, anyone who was converted from scepticism to a "liberal" or "demythologised" Christianity? I think that when unbelievers come in at all, they come in a good deal further.

Not, of course, that either group is to be judged by its success, as if the question were one of tactics. The liberals are honest men and preach their version of Christianity, as we preach ours, because they believe it to be true. A man who first tried to guess "what the public wants," and then preached that as Christianity *because* the public wants it, would be a pretty mixture of fool and knave.

I am enlarging on this because even you, in your last letter, seemed to hint that there was too much of the supernatural in my position; especially in the sense that "the next world" loomed so large. But how can it loom less than large if it is believed in at all?

You know my history. You know why my withers are quite unwrung by the fear that I was bribed—that I was lured into Christianity by the hope of everlasting life. I believed in God before I believed in Heaven. And even now, even if—let's make an impossible supposition—His voice, unmistakably His, said to me, "They have misled you. I can do nothing of that sort for you. My long struggle with the blind forces is nearly over. I die, children. The story is ending," would that be a moment for changing sides? Would not you and I take the Viking way: "The Giants and Trolls win. Let us die on the right side, with Father Odin."

But if it is not so, if that other world is once admitted, how can it, except by sensual or bustling pre-occupations, be kept in the background of our minds? How can the "rest of Christianity"—what is this "rest"?—be disentangled from it? How can we untwine this idea, if once admitted, from our present experience, in which, even before we believed, so many things at least *looked* like "bright shoots of everlastingness"?

And yet . . . after all. I know. It is a venture. We don't

know it will be. There is our freedom, our chance for a little generosity, a little sportsmanship.

Isn't it possible that many "liberals" have a highly illiberal motive for banishing the idea of Heaven? They want the gilt-edged security of a religion so contrived that no possible fact could ever refute it. In such a religion they have the comfortable feeling that, whatever the real universe may be like, they will not have "been had" or "backed the wrong horse." It is close to the spirit of the man who hid his talent in a napkin—"I know you are a hard man and I'm taking no risks." But surely the sort of religion they want would consist of nothing but tautologies?

About the resurrection of the body. I agree with you that the old picture of the soul re-assuming the corpse—perhaps blown to bits or long since usefully dissipated through nature —is absurd. Nor is it what St. Paul's words imply. And I admit that if you ask me what I substitute for this, I have only speculations to offer.

The principle behind these speculations is this. We are not, in this doctrine, concerned with matter as such at all; with waves and atoms and all that. What the soul cries out for is the resurrection of the senses. Even in this life matter would be nothing to us if it were not the source of sensations.

Now we already have some feeble and intermittent power of raising dead sensations from their graves. I mean, of course, memory.

You see the way my thought is moving. But don't run away with the idea that when I speak of the resurrection of the body I mean merely that the blessed dead will have excellent memories of their sensuous experience on earth. I mean it the other way round: that memory as we now know it is a dim foretaste, a mirage even, of a power which the soul, or rather Christ in the soul (He went to "prepare a place" for us), will exercise hereafter. It need no longer be intermittent. Above all, it need no longer be private to the soul in which it occurs. I can now communicate to you the fields of my boyhood—they are building-estates to-day— only imperfectly, by words. Perhaps the day is coming when I can take you for a walk through them.

At present we tend to think of the soul as somehow "inside" the body. But the glorified body of the resurrection as I conceive it—the sensuous life raised from its death—will be inside the soul. As God is not in space but space is in God.

I have slipped in "glorified" almost unawares. But this glorification is not only promised, it is already foreshadowed. The dullest of us knows how memory can transfigure; how often some momentary glimpse of beauty in boyhood is

> a whisper
> Which memory will warehouse as a shout.

Don't talk to me of the "illusions" of memory. Why should what we see at the moment be more "real" than what we see from ten years' distance? It is indeed an illusion to believe that the blue hills on the horizon would still look blue if you went to them. But the fact that they are blue five miles away, and the fact that they are green when you are on them, are equally good facts. Traherne's "orient and immortal wheat" or Wordsworth's landscape "apparelled in celestial light" may not have been so radiant in the past when it was present as in the remembered past. That is the beginning of the glorification. One day they will be more radiant still. Thus in the sense-bodies of the redeemed the whole New Earth will arise. The same, yet not the same, as this. It was sown in corruption, it is raised in incorruption.

I dare not omit, though it may be mocked and misunderstood, the extreme example. The strangest discovery of a widower's life is the possibility, sometimes, of recalling with detailed and uninhibited imagination, with tenderness and gratitude, a passage of carnal love, yet with no re-awakening of concupiscence. And when it occurs (it must not be sought) awe comes upon us. It is like seeing nature itself rising from its grave. What was sown in momentariness is raised in still permanence. What was sown as a becoming, rises as being. Sown in subjectivity, it rises in objectivity. The transitory secret of two is now a chord in the ultimate music.

"But this," you protest, "is no resurrection of the *body*. You give the dead a sort of dream world and dream bodies. They are not real." Surely neither less nor more real than those you have always known? You know better than I that the "real world" of our present experience (coloured, resonant, soft or hard, cool or warm, all corseted by perspective) has no place in the world described by physics or even by physiology. Matter enters our experience only by becoming sensation (when we perceive it) or conception (when we understand it). That is, by becoming soul. That element in the soul which it becomes will, in my view, be raised and glorified; the hills and valleys of Heaven will be to those you now experience not as a copy is to an original, nor as a substitute is to the genuine article, but as the flower to the root, or the diamond to the coal. It will be eternally true that they originated with matter; let us therefore bless matter. But in entering our soul as alone it can enter—that is, by being perceived and known—matter has turned into soul (like the Undines who acquired a soul by marriage with a mortal).

I don't say the resurrection of this body will happen at once. It may well be that this part of us sleeps in death, and the intellectual soul is sent to Lenten lands where she fasts in naked spirituality—a ghost-like and imperfectly human

123

condition. I don't imply that an angel is a ghost. But naked spirituality is in accordance with his nature; not, I think, with ours. (A two-legged horse is maimed, but not a two-legged man.) Yet from that fast my hope is that we shall return and re-assume the wealth we have laid down.

Then the new earth and sky, the same yet not the same as these, will rise in us as we have risen in Christ. And once again, after who knows what aeons of the silence and the dark, the birds will sing and the waters flow, and lights and shadows move across the hills, and the faces of our friends laugh upon us with amazed recognition.

Guesses, of course, only guesses. If they are not true, something better will be. For "we know that we shall be made like Him, for we shall see Him as He is."

Thank Betty for her note. I'll come by the later train, the 3:40. And tell her not to bother about a bed on the ground floor. I can manage stairs again now, provided I take them "in bottom." Till Saturday.

Books by C. S. Lewis
available from Harcourt Brace & Company
in Harvest paperback editions

ALL MY ROAD BEFORE ME: THE DIARY OF C. S. LEWIS, 1922–1927

THE BUSINESS OF HEAVEN: DAILY READINGS FROM C. S. LEWIS

THE DARK TOWER AND OTHER STORIES

THE FOUR LOVES

LETTERS OF C. S. LEWIS

LETTERS TO MALCOLM: CHIEFLY ON PRAYER

A MIND AWAKE: AN ANTHOLOGY OF C. S. LEWIS

NARRATIVE POEMS

OF OTHER WORLDS: ESSAYS AND STORIES

ON STORIES: AND OTHER ESSAYS ON LITERATURE

POEMS

PRESENT CONCERNS

REFLECTIONS ON THE PSALMS

SPIRITS IN BONDAGE: A CYCLE OF LYRICS

SURPRISED BY JOY: THE SHAPE OF MY EARLY LIFE

TILL WE HAVE FACES: A MYTH RETOLD

THE WORLD'S LAST NIGHT AND OTHER ESSAYS

Also available in Harvest paperback editions

C. S. LEWIS AT THE BREAKFAST TABLE AND OTHER REMINISCENCES,
edited by James T. Como

C. S. LEWIS: A BIOGRAPHY,
by Roger Lancelyn Green and Walter Hooper

THE LITERARY LEGACY OF C. S. LEWIS,
by Chad Walsh